Crystal and Fox
AND
The Mundy Scheme

Brian Friel

Crystal and Fox
AND
The Mundy Scheme

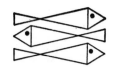

FARRAR, STRAUS AND GIROUX
New York

Published simultaneously in Canada by Doubleday Canada Ltd.,
Toronto

Printed in the United States of America

Crystal and Fox

A PLAY IN SIX EPISODES

To Sean McMahon

Characters

FOX MELARKEY
CRYSTAL MELARKEY, *his wife*
PAPA, *her father*
PEDRO
EL CID
TANYA, *Cid's wife*
GABRIEL, *Fox's son*
AN IRISH POLICEMAN
TWO ENGLISH DETECTIVES

FOX MELARKEY *is the proprietor of the traveling show that carries his name. He is about fifty, a small man, narrow-shouldered, lightly built, with a lean, sallow face grooved by a few deep wrinkles and patterned by a network of shallow wrinkles, a face that has been stamped with age since early manhood.*

CRYSTAL, *his wife, is a few years younger. She is taller than the Fox and heavier. She has a well-structured, peasant face, and on those rare occasions when she is groomed she has a fresh and honest attractiveness.*

PAPA, *Crystal's father, is in his late seventies. His voice is husky with age. He is almost totally deaf and shuffles around with his head down, doing his allotted chores with an almost desperate concentration: he is determined to be worthy of his keep.*

EL CID *and* TANYA, *a husband-and-wife team, are in their thirties. Their talent is limited, their self-confidence and optimism limitless.*

PEDRO *is sixty—a gentle and guileless man, untouched by the elations and depressions of his profession.*

There is an intermission after Episode 2.

The Set

The acting area is divided into two portions. The portion on the left (from the point of view of the audience) occupies about one-third of the area; the portion on the right, two-thirds. The dividing line is a flimsy, transparent framework that runs at an angle upstage. The portion left of this division is the *stage* inside Fox's marquee; the portion right is the *backstage;* the dividing framework is the *back wall* of the stage.

ACT ONE

EPISODE 1

AT RISE, *we join the Fox Melarkey Show during a brief interval before the final episode of their drama, "The Doctor's Story."*

CRYSTAL—*Mother Superior—is on her knees on the stage, her elbows resting on a chair. She is wearing a nun's white tropical habit that could do with a wash.*

EL CID—*Dr. Giroux—is backstage. He is wearing a short white medical coat. He is helping* TANYA—*Sister Petita Sancta—out of a nun's habit and into a gaudy floral dress.*

PAPA, *their stage manager, is pumping a Primus stove.*

FOX *is bustling around, trying to get his cast organized. He is on edge because from offstage left can be heard the slow clapping of an unseen audience and the chanting of "We want Fox! We want Fox!" The audience is restless and not very respectful; they have long since grown tired of suspending their disbelief. In a circle around the Primus stove are some upturned boxes and some props. Fox's piano accordion is in the wings.*

FOX

Come on! Come on! They're getting tired. What the hell's up now? Cid? Tanya?

TANYA

Just a minute, Fox.

FOX

Jaysus, will you hurry!

CID

Keep your hair on.

CRYSTAL

A good house, my sweet. A few weeks of this and we'll be able to trade in the truck.

FOX

(*Automatically*) Beautiful, my love. (*He kisses her on the forehead.*) Very moving. Gets me here (*heart*) every time.

CRYSTAL

My Fox.

FOX

(*To* ALL) They're a noisy pack of bailiffs, so belt it out a bit more. Plenty of guts.

PAPA

(*To* FOX) What's my name?

FOX

(*To* CRYSTAL) What's Papa's name?

CRYSTAL

(*To* FOX) Sean O'Sullivan.

FOX

(*To* PAPA) Sean O'Sullivan.

PAPA

Sean O'Sullivan.

CRYSTAL

(*To* FOX) From outside Dublin.

FOX

(*To* PAPA) From outside Dublin.

PAPA

(*To* FOX) What am I doing here?

FOX

Who the hell's going to ask you that! You—you—you're training for the Olympics!

PEDRO's *head appears.*

PEDRO

What's the holdup, Fox?

FOX

Our little missionary here (TANYA). Ready yet?

TANYA

One more second, Fox—

FOX

As far as I'm concerned, you can take a week at it; but there happen to be people out there—

CID

The lady asked for one second.

FOX

The who?

CID

Look, Melarkey, if you don't watch that tongue of yours—

CRYSTAL

Fox, go out and quieten them. Tell them a story.

FOX *surveys his company with distaste.*

FOX

If they're restless, tell them a story! Christ! (*Then switching on his professional smile, he swings out onto the stage and acknowledges his boisterous reception.*) Thank you, thank you, thank you very much, ladies and gentlemen. You have been a wonderful audience and it's a great pleasure for the Fox Melarkey Show to be back again in Ballybeg—

VOICE

Whose pleasure?

FOX

Who let my mother-in-law in here?

Laughter.

But it's wonderful to see you all again, and you've been very appreciative of our little show; and tomorrow night at the same time—

VOICE

What about the raffle?

FOX

Look at what's shouting about the raffle! Scrounged a penny from the child behind him so that he could go halves in his wife's twopenny ticket!

Laughter.

Keep calm, spendthrift: the raffle's coming immediately after this last episode of our little drama.

VOICE

Is it faked?

FOX

'Course it's faked!

Laughter.

And the word's fixed. Can't even speak English, that fella. Must be one of those Gaelic speakers from the back of the hills. I didn't tell you, did I, about his brother, Seamus, the one that never heard a word of English until he left school? Got a job in a drapery shop in Killarney. And the boss said to him, "Let's hear how you'd talk to the customers." "Musha, sir, me English, sir, sure it do be weak. Me jacket, sir? Am I right? And me breeches—and me shirt? Ah sure don't worry, sir; I do have all the right words up here (*indicating his head*) in me ass."

Laughter.

And now, ladies and gentlemen, the final episode in our little drama, "The Doctor's Story." (*He bows briefly, retreats behind the curtain, and has a quick look around.*) Bloody cowboys! Ready?

CRYSTAL
Ready.

FOX
Tanya?

TANYA
Go ahead.

FOX

Belt it out. And plenty of tears. All the hoors want is a happy ending. Okay, Papa; take it up.

PAPA *hoists up the curtain.* FOX *stands in the wings.* CRYSTAL *buries her face in her hands and prays.* TANYA *enters the set and knocks on the framework.*

TANYA

Mother.

CRYSTAL *is lost in prayer.*

Mother Superior.

CRYSTAL

Did someone call me?

TANYA

It's me, Mother. Sister Petita Sancta.

CRYSTAL *does not turn around.*

CRYSTAL

Ah, Petita, Petita, come in, my child.

TANYA

I'll come back later, Mother.

CRYSTAL

No, no, no. Come on in. I was just talking to God about all our little problems in our mission hospital here at Lakula in Eastern Zambia. (*She blesses herself and rises. She now faces her visitor.*)

CRYSTAL

But is it—? Yes, it is my Petita! Heavens bless me, I didn't recognize you in those clothes. Oh, my child, you look so fresh and sweet.

TANYA

The wife of the vice-consul presented it (*dress*) to me gratuitously.

CRYSTAL

Dear Petita. We're going to miss you so much here. But then our loss is Dr. Alan Giroux's gain.

TANYA

He is bidding—

She breaks off because the kettle on the stove has boiled and is whistling shrilly. FOX *hisses at* PAPA—*who does not hear him. So* FOX *dashes to the kettle and lifts it off.*

CRYSTAL

Indeed, our loss is Dr. Alan Giroux's gain.

TANYA

He is bidding farewell to the other sisters. Just reflect, Mother: this time tomorrow, he and I shall be in Paris! Ah, here he comes!

EL CID *enters. He is a professional magician: acting is not his most fluent talent.*

CID

I am here to say adieu, mon mère superior.

CRYSTAL

Dear, dear Dr. Giroux.

CID

I have just had a quick run round the children's, casualty, fever, and maternity wards. All is shipshape and Bristol fashion for my replacement, Dr. Karl Krauger, when he arrives at noon tomorrow. And, just to forestall any emergency, I gave every patient a double injection of streptomycin.

CRYSTAL

May God reward you, my son.

CID

You know I do not believe in your God, Mother.

CRYSTAL

Some day you will, Doctor. I have my sisters praying for you.

He laughs a skeptic's laugh.

TANYA

I shall pray too.

CRYSTAL

And now would you mind if an old woman gave you both her blessing?

TANYA *looks appealingly to* CID.

TANYA

For my sake, Alan.

CID

If it makes you happy, mon amour.

They kneel at CRYSTAL's *feet. In the wings,* FOX *has lifted his accordion and plays throbbing churchy chords as* CRYSTAL *prays.*

CRYSTAL

May God reward you both for your years of dedication to our little mission hospital here in Lakula in Eastern Zambia. May you both find the joy and happiness and content you deserve so richly. And if ever you feel like coming back to us, singly or doubly, our arms will be open wide to hold you to my bosom. My children.

TANYA
Thank you, Mother.

CID *and* TANYA *rise. A long, uneasy pause.*

CRYSTAL
Listen—the river boat.

PAPA *has missed his cue.* FOX *dashes over to one of the upturned boxes, grabs a whistle, and pumps a whooping sound from it.*

Yes, I knew I heard the river boat. (*Arms out*) Au revoir, mon enfants. (*She embraces them both.* CID *manfully brushes back a tear.*)

CID
Some day, Mother, I'll . . . I'll . . . (*He cannot trust himself to speak. He grabs* TANYA *by the hand and together they run off.*)

CRYSTAL
Goodbye . . . goodbye . . .

She sinks to her knees, joins her hands, and lifts her face up to heaven. It is a face of suffering and acceptance. PAPA *lowers the curtain. There is sporadic clapping.* FOX *moves around briskly, dispensing tired compliments, while the artists change costume for their final appearance.*

FOX

Very nice . . . beautiful work . . . very moving . . . lovely show.

TANYA

The line is "Oh, my child, you look so young and so beautiful"—but you're too damn bitchy to say that!

CRYSTAL

Sorry, love; I meant to say that—I really did—and—

CID

That damned old fool—(PAPA)—he makes that kettle whistle on purpose just to throw me!

FOX

Okay, okay, let's get changed, good work all round, very convincing, very pathetic, where's Pedro?

PEDRO *enters. In his arms he carries Gringo, his performing dog. She is dressed in a green skirt and green, matching hat.*

PEDRO

Here, boss.

FOX

(*To* CRYSTAL, *with casual intimacy*) Exquisite, my love.
(*He kisses her.*)

CRYSTAL

My pet?

FOX

My sweet. (*Aloud*) Everybody ready?

CID

Just a minute, Fox—don't forget our agreement.

FOX

Nice performance, Cid.

CID

Me and Tanya take the last call. Agreed?

FOX

Agreed. (*Aloud*) All set?

CID

It's understood then, Fox? We're agreed on that?

FOX

Anything you say. (*Aloud*) All standing by? Right. Up
she goes, Papa.

CID

Remember, Fox! I'm not asking you again!

PAPA *hoists up the curtain. The others wait in the wings.* FOX *is wearing his accordion. He is greeted by the same uncertain enthusiasm.*

FOX

Thank you, thank you, thank you. And now once more I'd ask you to show your appreciation of the top-rank artistes who performed on these boards tonight. Ireland's best-known and best-loved man of mystery and suspense—El Cid, and his beautiful assistant, Tanya! (*He strikes a heralding chord. Thin clapping from the audience.*)

Pause.

CID

Bastard! (*Then he catches* TANYA'*s hand and, assuming a radiant smile, he runs on.*)

FOX

Thank you, Tanya; thank you, El Cid. And now that dashing Spaniard and his team of superhuman dogs—the ex-star of the Moscow Circus—Pedro!

Another chord. Applause. PEDRO *enters, taking the dog with him.*

FOX

And lastly and by no means least, the lady whose musical and Thespian arts held us all in thrall tonight—I give you—my charming and devoted wife—the gracious Crystal Melarkey.

Another chord. Applause. CRYSTAL *skips on.*

And now for our raffle for the five-pound note. Would you, my love . . . ?

CRYSTAL

My Fox. And thank you, ladies and gentlemen. If you have your tickets ready, we'll get some little boy or girl to draw from this box. Have we a volunteer? Come on, children; don't be shy. What about that little lady down there?

FOX

Nobody in Ballybeg needs a fiver! (*This is greeted by hooting and laughter.*)

CRYSTAL

If you're all too shy, perhaps Pedro would be kind enough to draw for us. Pedro?

PEDRO *draws and hands her a ticket.*

A pink ticket; and the number is eighty-seven—eight seven. Would the lucky holder of ticket number 87 please come up for his prize.

PAPA *approaches from the audience, wearing a top coat and hat.*
FOX *strikes a chord. Applause, led by* CRYSTAL.

FOX

Give him a big hand, friends.

CRYSTAL

What is your name, sir?

PAPA

(*By rote*) My name is Sean O'Sullivan and I come from outside Dublin.

FOX

(*To audience*) Is he courting a Ballybeg girl?

Laughter.

CRYSTAL

Can I see your ticket? (*After checking*) And he is absolutely correct! Mr. Sean O'Sullivan from outside Dublin is the lucky winner!

FOX *hands over the money.*

FOX

Don't sicken yourself with ice pops, sonny.

CRYSTAL

Congratulations, sir.

FOX *strikes up an introduction to their theme song, "A-hunting we will go," and the company link arms and do a simple dance routine as they sing.*

ALL

A-hunting we will go,
A-hunting we will go.
We'll catch a fox and put him in a box.
A-hunting we will go.
Tantiffy tantiffy tantiffy,
A-hunting we will go.

FOX

Tomorrow's our last night in Ballybeg. Same time, same place, children under seven admitted free. A complete new variety show, another lucky raffle, and by popular demand a repeat of tonight's classical drama, "The Doctor's Story." See you again tomorrow. God bless.

They strike up the chorus again. By now PAPA *has returned and lowers the curtain. The thin clapping dies away quickly.*

CRYSTAL

The tide's turned! I told you, my love, didn't I?

FOX

(*Flat*) You did indeed.

CID

Melarkey!

FOX *is fully aware of* CID's *rage but completely ignores it. He goes very calmly, almost gently, to* PAPA *to recover the fiver. Then he changes into his ordinary clothes.*

FOX

Thanks, Papa. Nice performance.

CID

I'm talking to you, Melarkey!

TANYA

Easy, Cid.

CID

You promised! You said it was agreed!

TANYA

Don't lose control, Cid. Please don't.

CID

I gave you every warning! But that's okay! That suits me fine. I mean to say—money and conditions—I can rough it as good as the next. But when a man's professional standing is spit on by a weasel like that . . . !

FOX

Atta girl, Gringo. Worth your weight in gold. Eh?

CRYSTAL

My Fox . . .

TANYA

We'll talk about it after we've changed.

CID

There's been enough talk. He promised me—it was agreed—we take the last call. But I know him—watched him since I joined this lousy fit-up—twisted, that's what he is—twisted as a bloody corkscrew! No wonder his own son cleared off to England!

TANYA

Please, Cid—

CID

And I'll tell you something more about him: he's not going to stop until he's ratted on everybody! I know that character!

TANYA

(*To* FOX) He's upset Fox. His stomach curdles on him. (*To* CRYSTAL) In the morning he'll be—

CID

In the morning I'll be signed up with Dick Prospect's outfit! (*As he leaves*) And I'll tell you another thing about him: it won't be long before he's back where he began—touting round the fairs with a rickety wheel! (*He rushes off.* TANYA *knows she must go with him.*)

TANYA

I gave him bacon for his tea. It always gripes him . . .
(*She hesitates uncertainly—then rushes off.*)

CRYSTAL

Tanya! (*To* OTHERS) He doesn't mean it, does he?

No one speaks. She turns to FOX. *On occasions like this, his eyes go flat and he hides behind a mask of bland simplicity and vagueness.*

You're not letting him go, are you?

FOX

What's that?

CRYSTAL

Cid and Tanya! You're not going to let them walk away like that?!

PEDRO

If it's only the calls, Fox, Gringo and me, we don't give a damn; we'll come on first.

CRYSTAL

Fox!

FOX

My love?

CRYSTAL

They're really leaving!

FOX

Are they?

CRYSTAL

Go after them! Speak to them!

FOX

What about, my sweet?

CRYSTAL

For God's sake, we can't afford to lose them! I know he's difficult—but he's a good act. And if they go, that's twenty minutes out of the variety. And we've no play, Fox!

FOX

No play?

CRYSTAL

Without Cid! Without Tanya! What's got into you? Last month it was Billy Hercules. And before that it was the Fritter twins. Fox, I'm asking you.

FOX

What?

CRYSTAL

Just speak to him.

PEDRO

Maybe if I had word with Tanya—

CRYSTAL

It has to be the Fox. (*Pleading*) My love—

FOX

My sweet.

CRYSTAL

Say you're sorry—say anything you like—blame me, I don't care; but we must hold on to him.

FOX

No, no; couldn't blame you, my love.

CRYSTAL

I'm asking you—for my sake—go after them.

FOX

Couldn't do that, my love.

CRYSTAL

But they'll leave if you don't.

FOX

Will they?

CRYSTAL

My Fox! We need them.

FOX

That's true.

CRYSTAL

Then do something. You don't want them to leave us too, do you?

FOX *gives her a most pleasant smile.*

FOX

If I knew a simple answer to that, my Crystal, I'd go in for telling fortunes.

BRING DOWN LIGHTS

EPISODE 2

When the lights go up, CRYSTAL *and* PEDRO, *now out of costume, are sitting disconsolately on upturned boxes. They have been drinking tea.* CRYSTAL *is brooding over the departure of* CID *and* TANYA. PEDRO *is trying to be cheerful.*

PEDRO

It was in a pub just outside Galway, in the middle of last summer. Cid was there, and me and Billy Hercules and Tanya. And he comes in with this big red face of his and a tart with him and he says, "The drinks are on Dick Prospect, the biggest traveling show in Ireland!" So we says nothing, and he sits himself beside me and he says, "How's the Fox these times?" "Fine," I says. "Haven't run into him for years. And Crystal? Give her my love," he says and he laughs and gives the tart a dig with his elbow. "And the lad—what's this his name is?" "Gabriel," says I. "That's it. How's he shaping in the business?" So I never says a word to that: what the bugger didn't know did him no harm. And the next thing, out of the blue: "Pedro," says he, "I'll make you an offer: leave the Fox and come with me and you can name your own price." And everybody stopped talking. And I just put down the glass and I says to him, "Twenty years ago the Fox Melarkey gave me a job when no other show in the country would touch me," I says. "And the day I leave the Fox will be the day I'm not fit to do my piece." And d'you know what he done, Crystal? He gave me a shove and he says, "You're a fool—that's what you are, a fool." And he threw the big bull head back and laughed. God, he's a cheeky bugger, isn't he?

CRYSTAL
  Mm?

PEDRO
  Dick Prospect—he's a cheeky bugger.

CRYSTAL
  That's right, Pedro.

PAPA *enters. There are four untouched tea cups on the ground. He points to them.*

PAPA
  What's keeping Cid and Tanya?

PEDRO
  They're gone.

PAPA

(*To* CRYSTAL) What's he say?

PEDRO

Left.

PAPA

Left?

PEDRO *nods.* PAPA *shrugs his shoulders, lifts one cup, and sits sipping.*

PEDRO

Good house tonight, wasn't it?

CRYSTAL

That's the point—the same all last week—things were beginning to pick up! I told him that! Another month like this and we could have got a new truck. Now—! Honest to God, Pedro, I can't see what's going to happen.

PEDRO

He has his ways—like the rest of us.

CRYSTAL

You don't have to defend him to me, Pedro. And you know what I'm talking about. You've seen him.

PEDRO

It's only in the past few years.

CRYSTAL

Just before Gabriel went away; that's when it began.

PEDRO

Eight—ten years ago—my God (*with genuine enthusiasm and pride*), he was on top of his form then! Cracking jokes, striding about, giving orders like a king; and everywhere he went, Gabby perched up there on top of his shoulders! My God, the Fox Melarkey Show was a real show then!

CRYSTAL

Wasn't it, though?

PEDRO

He had the country in the palm of his hand!

CRYSTAL

That won't pay the bills now.

PEDRO

If he put his mind to it, he could build it up again. He could! Not a showman in the country to touch him!

CRYSTAL

For God's sake, look around you, man. Holes in the roof. Broken seats. And when the truck falls apart, what's going to pull the vans?

PEDRO

I've got a couple of quid put by, Crystal . . . there's not much in it . . . and there's only me and Gringo to spend it . . . and if it's any use . . .

CRYSTAL

Good Pedro.

PEDRO

Well, you know it's there and all you have to do is . . .

He breaks off because he hears FOX *approach.* FOX *swings on, singing, full of bounce and good spirits. He has a paper under his arm.*

FOX

There is a happy land far, far away
Where we get bread and jam four times a day . . .

(*Speaks*) D'you believe that, Pedro, eh? Move over in the bed and let an honest man in at his work.

PEDRO

You're looking very happy.

FOX

Me? Oh, just a simple man's satisfaction at the end of a good day's work. Another step closer to paradise. Is there nothing for the Fox?

CRYSTAL *ungraciously thrusts a cup in front of him.*

FOX

Thank you, my love. And then, of course, we've lost our young couple, Sir Cid and Dame Tanya, off to a pressing engagement in Stratford. "This time tomorrow he and I shall be in Paris." Jaysus, if I had to listen to that again, I'd shoot myself.

PAPA

(*To* FOX) They're gone.

FOX

Gone, but not forgotten, Papa.

PAPA

That's the way—here today, gone tomorrow.

FOX

Very true, Papa. (*Turns to* CRYSTAL) Your father's a real sage, my sweet: nothing ruffles him any more. All clowns become sages when they grow old, and when young sages grow old, they turn into clowns. I was an infant sage—did you know that, Pedro?

PEDRO

Have they left—Cid and Tanya?

FOX

(*With bitter smile*) In this company, you discuss a thing—
Jaysus—for half an hour, and then someone asks you
what you're talking about. Round and round in circles.
Same conversations, same jokes, same yahoo audiences;
just like your Gringo, Pedro, eh?—doing the same old
tricks again and again, and all you want is a little cube of
sugar as a reward. How many tons of sugar have you given
to bloody dogs over the past twenty, thirty years? Eh?

PEDRO

I couldn't even—

FOX

(*Still smiling*) And how do you know that one night
when there's a sudden moon that lights up the whole coun-
tryside brilliantly for a second—it comes out from behind
a cloud and for that second everything's black and white—
how do you know that, on a night like that, Gringo
wouldn't give you all the sugar cubes in the world for just
one little saucer of arsenic? Answer me that, Pedro.

CRYSTAL

Leave him alone.

FOX

He loves the dog—he really does—and all I want to know
is, does he love him that much that he'd—

CRYSTAL

Leave Pedro alone!

FOX *makes a florid gesture of obedience to her.*

FOX

My queen. (*To* PEDRO) Contentment lies in total obedi-ence—St. Paul's epistle to the South Africans.

He opens the paper and looks through it. Pause. CRYSTAL *rises and crosses to* PAPA. *She speaks into his ear.*

CRYSTAL

You should go to bed.

PAPA

I'm not a baby.

CRYSTAL

Do you want a hot-water bottle?

PAPA

Hate them things.

FOX

(*Reads for general amusement*) "The local Grand Opera Society held its annual meeting last Wednesday in Sweeney's Hotel in Drung. It was agreed to do Faust next April. There are four members in the Society."

PEDRO

Where's Drung?

FOX

County Tyrone; not far from where I first met my Crystal. The month of May.

CRYSTAL

June.

FOX

No, no, my love; it was the twelfth day of a glorious May. And the Fox was cycling out to make his fortune in the world with nothing but his accordion and his rickety wheel and his glib tongue, when what did he spy at the edge of the road but three snow-white horses and three golden vans.

CRYSTAL

(*To* PEDRO) The vans were brown.

FOX

And there was no one in the first golden van. And there was no one in the second golden van. But beside the third and last golden van there was Papa rubbing down a snow-white mare. And beside him a princess. And she had her hair tied up with a royal-blue ribbon, and a blue blouse, and a navy skirt—

CRYSTAL

(*Gruffly, with embarrassment*) You're a blatherskite.

FOX

—and a broach here with "MOTHER" written across it.

CRYSTAL

(*With sudden simplicity*) That's true!

FOX

And Papa was wearing puttees; and there was a smell of heather; and the mare's name was Alice.

CRYSTAL

Alice it was!

FOX

(*Quietly*) And I got off my bicycle—I had no idea what I was going to say; and Papa went on rubbing the mare. And the princess looked at me.

Pause.

PEDRO

What happened, Fox? By God, you weren't stuck for a word!

FOX

(*Briskly again*) And the Fox whipped off his cap and bowed low and said, "What big eyes you've got."

CRYSTAL

I fell on my feet that day.

FOX

Did you?

CRYSTAL

Take your tea, you eejit, you!

PEDRO

(*To* CRYSTAL) And then you and him and Papa set up on your own—after you got married?

CRYSTAL

We had more courage than sense.

FOX

And more hope than courage, my love.

PEDRO

By God, you were going great guns altogether when you took me on.

FOX

And aren't we still, Pedro? (*Deliberately finishing off the conversation*) Listen to this—something I saw here—about the caves at Knockmore—we could make it in a day, couldn't we? Here we are. (*Reads*) "Four young American students trapped in underground caves at Knockmore."

PEDRO

By God, those Americans are everywhere these times.

FOX

"So far, rescue teams have been unable to get to the young people who have been cut off since the entrance to the largest cave became blocked by falling boulders."

CRYSTAL

Any crowds gathering?

FOX

Doesn't say.

CRYSTAL

I still think we should head towards Dublin.

PEDRO

They don't flock to the tragedies the way they used to.

CRYSTAL

Television has them spoiled. It needs to be something very big.

PEDRO

A train crash or an explosion in a school.

FOX

Has to be children. Remember the time that orphanage in the Midlands burned down?

PEDRO

That sort of thing.

CRYSTAL

For three solid weeks, not an empty seat.

PEDRO

Marvelous.

CRYSTAL

And a matinee every other day.

PEDRO

But your chances of being actually on the spot—once in a lifetime.

PAPA

(*Rising*) I'd better put on the parking lights in the truck.

CRYSTAL

I'll see to it, Papa.

PAPA

What's that?

CRYSTAL

I'll do it.

PAPA

Don't forget. I'm away to bed, then. Good night all.

CRYSTAL

Sleep well, Papa.

PEDRO

'Night, Papa.

FOX

Good night, Papa. (*Suddenly*) Oh, Papa, Papa!

PAPA *stops.* FOX *fumbles in his pocket.*

The day before yesterday—remember when I was going into the town?—you gave me a shilling to put on a horse for you.

PAPA

Did I?

FOX

Planter's Delight in the 3.30. It romped home at nine to one. Here's your winnings.

PAPA'*s face lights up with joy.*

PAPA

I forgot all about it . . . isn't that a good one, eh? . . . went clean out of my head . . . ten shillings, eh? . . . good man, Fox.

PEDRO

Maybe you're set for a lucky streak, Papa.

PAPA

Clean out of my head . . . bloody good man, Fox.

FOX

You can still pick them, Papa!

PAPA

Bloody good . . . (*Leaves.*)

PEDRO

That's the first win he's had in months. There'll be no stopping him now.

CRYSTAL

You weren't in the town the day before yesterday.

FOX

Papa got his winnings, didn't he? He's happy, isn't he? (*Changing the subject*) Here—look at that. (*Stares at* PEDRO's *hands.*)

PEDRO

What are you staring at?

FOX

Just a thought.

PEDRO

What does that mean? What sort of a thought?

FOX

Look at those hands, my pet.

CRYSTAL

Whose hands?

FOX

Pedro's.

PEDRO *puts his hands behind his back like a child.*

No—no—hold them out—let's look at them.

PEDRO *brings them out reluctantly.*

PEDRO

What's wrong with them?

FOX

That's it—turn them over—look at them.

CRYSTAL

What, Fox?

FOX

The long, slender fingers—the strength of them.

PEDRO

They're clean, aren't they?

FOX

Never noticed it before.

PEDRO

Now you're making them shake!

FOX

There's your man. The problem's solved.

PEDRO

Who?—what?—what are you talking about?

FOX

The hands of a surgeon. There's your Dr. Alan Giroux.

CRYSTAL

Our Pedro?

FOX

A natural.

PEDRO

A natural what?—what problem?

CRYSTAL

I don't know, Fox; he's—

FOX

I do. I'm sure of it. Absolutely perfect.

CRYSTAL

Would you, Pedro?

PEDRO

Would I what?

FOX

'Course he would.

CRYSTAL

Cid's part in the play—the young French doctor.

PEDRO

Me?!

CRYSTAL

(*To* FOX) Maybe he's—

PEDRO

Me? Me in the play? Christ, you're not serious! Me? Sure I can't even introduce my own act! Come on, Fox, cut it out—none of that sort of talk! Crystal, you know, Crystal, Christ Almighty, I couldn't! For God's sake have a heart, man! Don't ask it of me!

CRYSTAL

He doesn't want to, Fox. Anyway, we'd still have no Petita.

PEDRO

I'd do anything to pull you out of a hole, Fox—anything—you know that—but, Christ, acting a part! Dogs is all I can handle—I'm nothing without a dog—you know that, Crystal.

FOX

Okay. Shut up. Stop bleating.

PEDRO

If it was anything else, Fox—

FOX

Forget it.

PEDRO

You know, Crystal—

FOX

Forget it! Stop whining about it! Papa'll play it!

FOX's *outburst creates an embarrassed silence. He goes back to his paper.* PEDRO *looks appealingly to* CRYSTAL, *but she is not looking at him. Pause.*

CRYSTAL

It's time we all went to bed.

She begins to gather up the tea things.
No one has noticed the entrance of a motorcycle POLICEMAN *in helmet, goggles, gauntlets, riding breeches, leather knee-boots.*

He stands motionless, slowly surveying every detail. His silent presence generates an immense threat. When he speaks, his voice is soft and controlled.

FOX *glances over his paper and sees him first. Immediately he switches on his best manner, but his garrulousness betrays his unease.*

FOX

Good night, Sergeant! Visitors, my love! You're a bit late for the show, Sergeant, but you're just in time for a cup of tea. Tea for the gentleman, my love.

The POLICEMAN *moves silently around.*

Wait a minute—didn't I see you at the show tonight?—in civvies—standing down at the back. Amn't I right, boss? It was the goggles there that threw me for a—

POLICEMAN
Fox Melarkey?

FOX

At your service, Sergeant. Have a pew. Take the weight off your legs.

Silence. The POLICEMAN *stands before* PEDRO.

POLICEMAN
Who are you?

FOX

(*Before* PEDRO *can reply*) That's Pedro, boss. A wizard
with dogs. One of the top artists in the profession. Been
with the Fox Melarkey Show for the best part of—

POLICEMAN

Can you speak? What's your name?

PEDRO

Paddy Donnellan. Pedro's the name I use for the show.

FOX

And this is the better half—Crystal—Mrs. Fox Melarkey—
or the vixen, as I sometimes call her!

The POLICEMAN *ignores him.*

POLICEMAN

Who else is there?

FOX

You mean who else is there in the company, boss? Well,
there's Papa, that's Crystal's father—he's just gone to bed—
the old ticker's liable to jack up on him without warning—
as a matter of fact, you just missed him by a few seconds—
great character—was a clown all his days—toured with
some of the biggest outfits in Europe. And there's . . . and
there's . . . damnit, that's it! An hour ago we had another
pair, man and wife team; but they upped and offed on me

without as much as by your leave. You've no idea, boss, what it's like trying to cater to top-quality artistes these days with competition from TV and—

POLICEMAN

Only four? No one else?

FOX

That's it, Sergeant. Just four—for the time being. We'll just have to say our prayers and tour the agents again. No want of talent round the country, boss, as a gentleman in your position knows well; but when your audiences are made up of decent country people and their little kiddies, you just can't sign up every cheapjack that wants to join you.

POLICEMAN

No one else in the vans?

CRYSTAL

If you don't take his word, why don't you search them?

FOX

No one else, Sergeant. Not a soul. Just the four of us: Crystal, Pedro, Papa, and yours truly. As Shakespeare says, "We are a few and a happy few and a band of brothers"—

POLICEMAN

When are you moving out?

FOX

When are we moving out? Isn't that a coincidence—the very thing we were talking about when you arrived! Right, my pet? I'll tell you our problem, boss. We could do another week, ten days here easy. Jaysus, if we turned away five the night, we must have turned away—what would you say, my love?—fifty? sixty? On the other hand, if we don't keep to our schedule, our advance agents start screaming at us—

POLICEMAN

When?

FOX

When? As a matter of fact, Sergeant, it was . . . it was the consensus of opinion that . . . that we honor our previous commitments and . . . and pull out tomorrow morning.

POLICEMAN

Make it early in the morning, so that you'll be outside my territory by noon.

CRYSTAL

Why should we?

FOX

Sure, boss, sure. Anything you say, Sergeant. Suits us fine. As a matter of fact, we've got to be in Ardbeg by tomorrow afternoon. The new hall there's at our disposal any time we want it. That's what we were just saying—can we make it in time. But we'll make it, boss; don't you worry; that's where we'll be. The Fox Melarkey never let his public down yet. Leave it to me, Sergeant. I'll handle it.

The POLICEMAN *pauses before leaving and looks at* CRYSTAL.

POLICEMAN

I'm just giving you good advice, missus. Pay heed to it.

FOX

And we're grateful for it, boss, very grateful. And now that you're here, you're the very man that can advise me on the best route. Should we go up through the gap or should we go round by the foot of Glenmore? It's so long since I did that trip that I've forgotten which is the quickest road . . . (*His voice fades away as he goes off with the* POLICEMAN.)

CRYSTAL

Gestapo!

PEDRO

He's after something, whatever it is.

CRYSTAL

The Fox is far too sweet to them fellas. I'd give them their answer.

PEDRO

No point in crossing them.

CRYSTAL

Out of his territory! You'd think he owned the place! You'd think we were criminals!

PEDRO

He's doing his job.

CRYSTAL

It's a dirty job, then. And I never could stomach them.

PEDRO

So we're moving out tomorrow?

CRYSTAL

Gestapo.

PEDRO

I say—looks as if we're moving out in the morning.

CRYSTAL

Why should we?

PEDRO

It was Fox—he said it—he said we were going to—

CRYSTAL

"He said—he said." If he had his way, we'd keep moving all the time and never light anywhere. Near time he made up his mind to run the show right or pack it in altogether.

CRYSTAL's *uncustomary sharpness embarrasses* PEDRO.

PEDRO

Well, I thought . . . maybe he only meant . . . Supper
time for Gringo.

CRYSTAL

I'd give them their answer.

PEDRO

'Night, Crystal.

*She does not hear him. She gathers up the tea things, making a
lot of noise in her agitation.*

GABRIEL *appears right and stands watching them. He is in his
early twenties. He has inherited a portion of* CRYSTAL's *forthright-
ness and a portion of* FOX's *depth and they make an uneasy mar-
riage in him. He gives a first impression of being weak—an impression that is not altogether accurate. He is wearing an anorak
and an open-necked shirt and carrying a sailor's duffel bag over
his shoulder.*

GABRIEL

(*Quietly, without intonation*) Any chance of a bed for the
night?

PEDRO

Crystal! Look! It's Gabriel!

CRYSTAL *turns round and stares incredulously.*

CRYSTAL

Gabriel? . . . Oh, my God—Gabriel! It's Gabriel—oh, my God! (*She runs to him and flings her arms round him.*)

GABRIEL

Crystal!

CRYSTAL

Son!

GABRIEL

Great to see you.

CRYSTAL

I heard Pedro—and I looked up—and whatever way the light was—!

GABRIEL

I wanted to surprise you.

CRYSTAL

And the size of him! Look at him, Pedro! A man big!

GABRIEL

Pedro!

PEDRO *and* GABRIEL *embrace.*

PEDRO

Welcome . . . Welcome back.

GABRIEL

It's great to be back! How are you all? Where's Papa? Where's Fox? Where is everybody?

CRYSTAL

Fox is about, and Papa's just gone to bed, and here's Pedro, and here's me! He's got so . . . so mannish-looking! When did you come? How did you find us?

GABRIEL

Crossed from Glasgow last night and hitched the rest of the way. Pedro! How's all the dogs, man?

PEDRO

Only one now—Gringo—

GABRIEL

One? Only one?

PEDRO

—but she—she's—I'll show her to you—hold on—

CRYSTAL

Not now. In the morning.

PEDRO

Never had a dog like her. She's . . . she's like a wife.

CRYSTAL

Papa'll be so excited, I'll tell him. No, I won't—he wouldn't sleep after.

GABRIEL

How's he keeping?

CRYSTAL

Not bad. Seventy-eight last month.

GABRIEL

(*Diffidently*) And the Fox?

CRYSTAL

Great. As ever. The same Fox. Fighting the world.

PEDRO

My God, wait till he sees you!

GABRIEL

Maybe I should . . . maybe you should tell him I'm here first, in case—

CRYSTAL

That was five years ago. It's all forgotten. He talks about you all the time—doesn't he?

PEDRO

Every day, twice a day.

GABRIEL

He threw me out, remember.

CRYSTAL

I'm telling you—he'll be delighted. Are you hungry? When did you last eat?

FOX *enters briskly. He does not see* GABRIEL.

FOX

Trust you to put the big feet in it! The truck sitting there not taxed and no parking lights and you have to give lip to the peeler! Only that I kept talking bloody quick— (*Now he sees* GABRIEL.)—It's not . . . ?

GABRIEL

The prodigal son, Fox.

FOX

Jaysus!

CRYSTAL

I told him you'd be—

FOX

Gabriel!

FOX *moves first towards him. They meet and embrace.* FOX *holds his son tightly. He is on the point of tears.*

GABRIEL

Easy, Fox, easy.

CRYSTAL

Isn't he looking great?

FOX

He's looking . . . divine. A lad went away—remember, Pedro?—and look, my sweet, a man, a man. And the presence—the style! When did he come?

CRYSTAL

Just now.

FOX

How did he find us?

GABRIEL

(*Deadpan*) Well, when I got off the ship this morning I bought an Irish paper and I looked to see were there any big catastrophies that would gather a crowd of sightseers; and I read that in County—

FOX

The hoor! Still at his bloody monkey-tricks! (*To* PEDRO) You always said he'd make a great clown. (*Softly*) Jaysus, but it's good to see you, son. After you went away, somehow we . . . we . . . But now you're back to us and suddenly life's . . . (*He breaks off; continues briskly*) How d'you think she's looking?

GABRIEL

No change.

FOX

No change at all. She is my constant enchantment. (*He kisses her.*)

CRYSTAL

My Fox.

FOX

And without her I am nothing. And Pedro?

GABRIEL

Not a day older.

PEDRO

Haa!

FOX

We survive.

CRYSTAL

And your father?

GABRIEL

The very same.

FOX

No, no.

GABRIEL

Maybe a bit heavier.

FOX

And more perverse and more restless and more . . .
You're the one that's put on weight.

GABRIEL

Too much beer. Where's the rest of the gang?

FOX

Crystal—Pedro—your humble servant—and Papa, of
course; you haven't seen Papa yet? He'll be glad to see you.
Well, that's about it. Things have changed since . . . since
you left. Nowadays if you're not compact, streamlined,
overheads cut to a minimum, you're out of business. Quick,
slick, first-rate. TV finished the shoddy show. But we've
been lucky; my sweet?

CRYSTAL

Very lucky.

FOX

Things have changed all right; audiences, artists. Strange.
You'd be surprised. And a man changes, too. You'd be surprised. The years do strange things to a man. But I have
my Crystal.

CRYSTAL

And Pedro.

PEDRO

I'll show you the dog later, Gabriel. She wears a green hat
and a green skirt.

GABRIEL

Can she count?

PEDRO

And read. She's uncanny.

CRYSTAL

She lies in the bed with him and eats at the table with him!

FOX

You're home to stay, aren't you?

Pause.

CRYSTAL

Even for a while.

GABRIEL

For a while—sure—why not.

PEDRO

We'll have a celebration! I've a bottle of whiskey since
Christmas that I haven't opened.

CRYSTAL

What about something to eat?

PEDRO

We'll drink first—then we'll eat. (*To* CRYSTAL) Have you any glasses?

CRYSTAL

I'll get some.

PEDRO

Come over to my van. Gringo'll want to be in on the fun. (*As he leaves*) It's like old times again. (*Goes off.*)

CRYSTAL

He's as excited as if you were his own child.

GABRIEL

Great guy.

CRYSTAL

We're all excited.

GABRIEL

I remember that smell: wet fields and paraffin and turf.

CRYSTAL

I knew the tide was turned—I said that—didn't I?

FOX

My love—glasses.

CRYSTAL

But we're round the corner now. I know we are. (*Goes off.*)

Now that FOX *and* GABRIEL *are alone, there is a diffidence between them: they are both conscious of it.*

GABRIEL

Same old stove.

FOX

It goes for no one but Papa.

GABRIEL

(*Avoiding conversation*) And that patch—(*on the roof*)— I remember helping Pedro to sew it. Must have been only nine or ten at the time. He was up on top of a stepladder and I was trying to hold it steady and it kept sinking into the ground and I was sure he was going to fall on top of me . . . but he didn't . . . How's business?

FOX

Good. Fair.

GABRIEL

Have things got rough?

FOX

No rougher than usual.

GABRIEL

But you're managing?

FOX

We've always managed. Sometimes you get sick managing. Smoke?

GABRIEL

Thanks.

FOX

(*With his brittle smile*) And we're getting on, Gabby boy; maybe that's it. Not as much spirit now.

GABRIEL

You're still a young man.

FOX

(*Pleasantly, almost casually*) Weary of all this . . . this making-do, of conning people that know they're being conned. Sick of it all. Not sick so much as desperate; desperate for something that . . . that has nothing to do with all this. Restless, Gabby boy, restless. And a man with a restlessness is a savage bugger.

GABRIEL

What do you want?

FOX

What do I want? I want . . . I want a dream I think I've had to come true. I want to live like a child. I want to die and wake up in heaven with Crystal. What do I want? Jaysus, man, if I knew the answer to that, I might be content with what I have. (*Without stopping*) I like your jacket.

GABRIEL

I never had any talent for this business. I would have been no help.

FOX

That row we had—

GABRIEL

Which one? We fought every other day. I was a cocky bastard.

FOX

You know the one I mean—the big one. I'm sorry about that . . . my fault. I would have written to you, but I didn't know—

GABRIEL

Forget it, Fox; for Christ's sake, forget it.

FOX

Well now I've said it.

GABRIEL

If I had a pound for every fight I've been in since, I'd be a rich man . . . a bloody millionaire. Been here long?

FOX

Just tonight.

GABRIEL

How is it?

FOX

Great—great.

GABRIEL

You'll stay, then?

FOX

Pulling out in the morning, as a matter of fact. Booking lined up in Ardmore. I tried to cancel it—phoned just before the show—but they're holding us to it.

GABRIEL

That sounds good. I think I remember Ardmore.

FOX

What have you been doing since?

GABRIEL

Me? Everything . . . nothing much . . . a bit of a drifter.

FOX

Were you at sea?

GABRIEL *touches the duffel bag with his foot.*

GABRIEL

For a while. And British Railways for a while. And dish-washing. And street photographer. Anything that came along. We're a restless breed, Fox.

FOX

You're not home to stay at all.

GABRIEL

Maybe. I don't know. Depends.

FOX

You're in trouble—isn't that it?

GABRIEL

Trouble?

FOX

With the police. Isn't that it?

GABRIEL

Takes a fox to know a fox. That's why we could never get on—we're too alike.

FOX

What's the trouble?

GABRIEL

When I was nabbed first—not long after I went over
there—they sent me to one of those psychiatrist blokes.
And do you know what he said, Fox? He said I was autistic—"unable to respond emotionally to people." Funny
word—autistic—isn't it? Got me off the hook a couple of
times.

FOX

The trouble.

GABRIEL

And this bloke kept asking me about the show and about
you and Crystal and the traveling around. Dead serious.
Make a good straight man.

FOX

Why are the police after you?

GABRIEL

were some sort of a softy and that Crystal was tough as
nails.

FOX

What did you do?

GABRIEL

Me? I—

CRYSTAL

(*Offstage*) Fox! Gabriel!

FOX

She's to know nothing.

GABRIEL

Do you think I'd tell her?

FOX

Tell me.

GABRIEL

I was in this digs. In Salford. And it was a Saturday night —last Saturday three weeks. And I had a bad day with the horses. And this bitch of a landlady, she kept shouting up for her money. And the bloke that shared the room with me, I owed him money too. So I gathered my things and dropped them out the window and then I went out to the yard and over the wall.

CRYSTAL

(*Offstage*) Come on, you two!

GABRIEL

We're missing the fun.

He got everything all wrong: he worked it out that you

FOX

Go on.

GABRIEL

Must have been nearly midnight by then. And about four streets away there was this newspaper shop and the old woman—she knew me—I used to go in there sometimes— she was closing up. And I asked her for a packet of fags and she said, "Hold on, love, till I put up these shutters." And when she went out to the front I saw the till was open. And there was no one about. And just as I reached my hand across, in she comes and starts clawing at me and screaming at me. I tried to shake her off and I couldn't. And she kept screaming and scratching at me. And I was terrified. And I caught this weight—I think it was on the scales—and I hit her. But that didn't stop her. So I hit her again. And again . . .

Pause.

FOX

Did you kill her?

GABRIEL

That's the point, Fox; I'm not sure.

FOX

Jaysus.

CURTAIN

INTERMISSION

ACT TWO

EPISODE 3

Early evening, a week later.

Backstage of the marquee: now it is pitched on a different site—the backstage is left.

A rehearsal is in progress. FOX *is kneeling, his elbows on a chair. He is wearing the habit—but not the headdress—that* CRYSTAL *wore at the opening of Episode 1. He is also wearing a large leather belt and hopes to look like a monk.*

FOX

(*Roars*) I'm not staying on my bloody knees all day! Will you hurry up!

CRYSTAL *appears at the door carrying a bucket of water.*

CRYSTAL

(*Sharply*) Someone has to carry the water, you know!

FOX

Surely! In the middle of a rehearsal? All right—all right; get a move on now.

CRYSTAL

'Cause if I don't go for it, none of the gentlemen around here would think of carrying it.

FOX

It's your entrance.

CRYSTAL

So just cool down. (*Very sweetly*) Father.

FOX *is lost in prayer.*

Father Superior.

FOX

Did someone call me?

CRYSTAL

It's me, Father. Sister Petita Sancta.

FOX *does not turn round.*

FOX

Ah, Petita, Petita, come in, my child.

CRYSTAL

I'll come back later, Father.

FOX

No, no, no. Come on in. I was just talking to God about all our little problems in our mission hospital here at Lakula in Eastern Zambia.

FOX *now rises and faces his visitor.*

But is it—? Yes, it is my Petita! Heavens bless me, I didn't recognize you in those clothes. Oh, my child, you look so young and so beautiful.

CRYSTAL
The wife of the vice-consul presented it to me gratuitously.

FOX
Dear Petita. We are going to miss you so much here. But then our loss is Dr. Alan Giroux's gain.

CRYSTAL
He is bidding farewell to the other sisters. Just reflect, Father: this time tomorrow he and I shall be in Paris! Ah, here he comes! Come on, Dr. Giroux!

PEDRO *runs on. He is wearing a short white medical coat. He is absolutely wretched.*

PEDRO
I have just had a quick run round—

FOX
"I am here to say adieu."

PEDRO
I am here to say adieu, mon mère superior.

FOX

Dear, dear Dr. Giroux.

PEDRO

I have just had a quick run round the children's, casualty, fever, and maternity wards. I gave every nun a double injection of streptomycin.

FOX

(*Wryly*) Why not! They're all drug addicts!

CRYSTAL

Let him go on, Fox. I'm late for the hospital as it is.

FOX

Okay, okay. May God reward you, my son.

PEDRO

You know I do not believe in your God, Fox—Father.

FOX

Some day you will, Doctor. I have my priests praying for you. (*Pause.*) Laugh.

PEDRO

I can't.

FOX

Try.

PEDRO *produces a strange sound.*

Cut the laugh.

CRYSTAL
I shall pray, too.

FOX
And now would you mind if an old man gave you both his blessing?

CRYSTAL
For my sake, Alan.

PEDRO
If it makes you happy, mon amour.

CRYSTAL *and* PEDRO *kneel.*

FOX
May God reward you both for your years . . . and so on and so on . . . Our arms will be open wide to hold you to our bosom—chest. My children.

GABRIEL *comes on and watches the rehearsal.*

CRYSTAL
Thank you, Father.

FOX
Toot-toot—listen—the riverboat.

PEDRO

Some day, Father, I'll—

FOX

Goodbye, goodbye. (*To* CRYSTAL) If you hurry, you'll still make it. (*To* PEDRO) Exquisite, Pedro. Very moving.

PEDRO

Fox, for the love of God—

FOX

A sincerity all his own; hasn't he, my love?

FOX *takes off his habit.* CRYSTAL *pulls on a coat.*

CRYSTAL

There's a bus around six. We'll be back on it.

PEDRO

I can't do it! And you know I can't do it!

FOX

You'll be fine, man. Don't worry.

CRYSTAL

Ready, Gabriel? Come on. Visiting time'll be over and Papa'll think we've forgotten him.

GABRIEL

Tell him I'll see him at the weekend.

CRYSTAL
You're not coming?

GABRIEL
Next Saturday—tell him next Saturday.

CRYSTAL
That's what you said last Saturday. You said you were coming today. You promised me, Gabriel.

GABRIEL
It's not—it's just . . . I'm not feeling so well.

CRYSTAL
And you're the only one he keeps asking for.

GABRIEL
Next weekend—tell him that. Next weekend for sure.

CRYSTAL
When did you get sick?

GABRIEL
It's a headache. I often get them.

CRYSTAL *looks to* FOX *for an explanation.*

FOX
(*Quickly*) You're going to miss the bus.

CRYSTAL

I don't understand it; that's all. And neither will he.

PEDRO

Tell him Gringo sent her love.

FOX

Have you the clean pajamas and the oranges?

CRYSTAL *nods.*

And tell him we can't hold a raffle until he comes back.

CRYSTAL

He (GABRIEL) could do the raffle.

FOX *takes a packet of cigarettes from his pocket, shakes them, and throws them to* CRYSTAL.

FOX

Here—give him these.

CRYSTAL

I'll be back before seven. (*Goes off.*)

FOX

(*Calling*) And tell him to keep his hands off the nurses. (*To* GABRIEL) The least you could do is go and see him before he dies.

GABRIEL *ignores him.*

I'm talking to you!

GABRIEL

(*Completely calm, almost indifferent*) You know I can't walk about.

FOX

She doesn't know that.

GABRIEL

It's a wonder you didn't tell her.

FOX

I didn't tell her—for her sake, not yours.

GABRIEL

If there was money in it, you wouldn't have kept so quiet, would you?

FOX

I'm not much, sonny, but I'm no informer.

PEDRO

Fox, I don't want to keep on about it—

FOX

What—what—what?

PEDRO

You don't know how miserable I am, doing this stuff.

FOX

Beautiful, Pedro. Exquisite.

PEDRO

I can't even pronounce the words right. (*Absolutely miserable*) Gabriel, would you . . . ?

GABRIEL

Ug-huh.

PEDRO

You'd be great—a young man and all.

GABRIEL

I won't be around much longer, Pedro.

PEDRO *shuffles off.*

PEDRO

All I know is, if I could see myself up there (*on stage*), I'd never lift my head again.

FOX *busies himself gathering up the props.* GABRIEL *and he are both conscious of the tension between them.*

GABRIEL

Do you want a hand?

FOX

No.

Pause.

GABRIEL

Isn't there a show tonight?

FOX

Unlikely.

GABRIEL

I thought you went around with handbills this morning?

FOX

I did.

GABRIEL

Well, if you put out bills—

FOX *interrupts him sharply and stands poised, listening.*

FOX

Shh!

GABRIEL

What is it?

Silence. FOX *relaxes and goes on working.*

FOX

Nothing.

GABRIEL

Crystal thinks there's a show. That's why she's rushing back. (*Pause.*) I didn't mean what I said—about you and money.

FOX

Doesn't matter.

GABRIEL

Well, what do you expect me to do? Go to the hospital with her and be picked up there? Is that what you want? All right, then; I'll go. And I'll tell her first—

FOX

She's not to know.

GABRIEL

She's going to know. If the old man dies and I haven't gone to see him—(*He breaks off because* CRYSTAL *enters.*)

FOX

What's wrong?

CRYSTAL

Missed it by a second. It went flying past just as I got to the road.

FOX

Come on. There's enough petrol in the truck to take us there and back.

CRYSTAL

And it not taxed? And all those peelers about the town?

FOX

It's insured. Isn't that enough for them? Come on—the old man'll be waiting.

GABRIEL

Crystal, I've something to tell you.

FOX

If nobody else is going, I'm going myself.

GABRIEL

I can't go anywhere, Crystal, because the police are after me.

CRYSTAL

Police?

FOX

It's nothing—nothing at all—

GABRIEL

I've been on the run for over a month.

CRYSTAL

What did you do?

FOX

He stole money from a shop—that's what he did—

GABRIEL

And there was an old—

FOX

He lifted a few shillings and bolted.

CRYSTAL

Where?

GABRIEL

Salford.

CRYSTAL

Where's that?

GABRIEL

Near Manchester.

CRYSTAL

How much?

GABRIEL

I don't know—£2—maybe £3—it's not the—

FOX

And then he ran and that's the whole story. I told him not to tell you. Can't keep his bloody mouth shut.

GABRIEL

I'll clear out in the morning—sign on with a tanker—

CRYSTAL *is very cool, very calm, very much in command.*

CRYSTAL

Is it the English police that are after you?

GABRIEL

I don't know. I think so.

CRYSTAL

Were you seen?

GABRIEL

I suppose so—

FOX

He was.

CRYSTAL

Have they got your name?

GABRIEL

I don't think so.

CRYSTAL

How much money did you lift?

GABRIEL

A few pounds—

CRYSTAL

How much?

GABRIEL

Four-ten.

CRYSTAL

When did this happen?

GABRIEL

About a month ago.

CRYSTAL

Where were you since?

FOX

Glasgow.

CRYSTAL

And then you came straight here to us?

GABRIEL

Yes.

CRYSTAL

Did you hang about Dublin?

GABRIEL

No. Look, I'll clear out tomorrow—

FOX

If we got him the length of Cork or Belfast, he could get a boat to—

CRYSTAL

He's going nowhere! We've been in trouble before; and the way to get out of it is to sit still and say nothing—to nobody! Is that clear? You can help with the show. You'll get some money. And as long as we keep on the move and steer clear of the towns, you're as safe as houses. Out of sight—out of mind—they'll soon forget about you. Is that clear?

GABRIEL *shrugs*. CRYSTAL *turns to* FOX.

Is that clear?

FOX

What if they come looking for him?

CRYSTAL

D'you think they're going to search the country for the sake of four pounds ten shillings? (*To* GABRIEL) It's up to you: stick with the show and keep your mouth shut and that'll be the end of it. Anyway, we could do with the help . . . I suppose it's near tea time.

GABRIEL

I'm sorry, Crystal.

CRYSTAL

Maybe this way you'll have to stay with us.

She goes wearily to the other end of the marquee and throws her coat across a seat. While she is outside their range:

FOX

(*Viciously*) You're a louse to have told her!

GABRIEL

She suspected.

FOX

And what are you going to tell her if they come for you? Eh?

GABRIEL

I would have told her the whole truth at the beginning.

FOX

That you may be wanted for murder?

GABRIEL

You leave me alone and I'll keep out of your way.

CRYSTAL *is back.*

CRYSTAL

We need some methylated for the stove. That was one of Papa's jobs.

FOX

He'll wonder nobody turned up.

CRYSTAL

There's visiting tomorrow. I'll get the early bus and—

She breaks off. PEDRO *has entered, carrying the lifeless body of* GRINGO *in his arms.* PEDRO *is so stunned that he is beyond emotion.*

PEDRO

It's Gringo.

CRYSTAL

Pedro—?

GABRIEL

Is she sick? She's not—?

CRYSTAL

What's wrong, Pedro? What's happened?

PEDRO
Gringo.

GABRIEL
Christ.

CRYSTAL
I saw her this morning after breakfast—she was fine—

GABRIEL
She's stiff.

CRYSTAL
Oh God.

GABRIEL *touches the dog's mouth.*

What—what's that stuff?

PEDRO
My Gringo.

GABRIEL
Must have been poisoned.

CRYSTAL
How could she have been poisoned, you fool! She never leaves the van!

PEDRO

And she's wise, very wise. And humorous, very humorous.

CRYSTAL

Oh God, Pedro, Pedro!

PEDRO

She'll be seven next birthday . . . tenth of March. I make a cake and put candles on it.

CRYSTAL

Is there nothing—? Brandy—?

GABRIEL

Dead a good while.

PEDRO

I called her. "Where are you?" I says. "I know you're hiding," I says. "I've got liver for your supper," I says. "And if you don't come out, I'll eat it all myself," I says. 'Cos I know she likes liver.

CRYSTAL *puts her arm around him. He moves off, very slowly. She goes with him.*

And I put it on the pan. And I thought the smell would coax her. And all the time I kept talking to her the way I always do . . .

CRYSTAL

Pedro.

PEDRO

And when there was no sign of her, I started looking for her. "I'll give you skelp," I says. "That's what you'll get— a right good skelp." 'Cos she knows I'd never lay a finger on her . . . (*His voice fades away.*)

GABRIEL

Christ, that's awful . . . She's all he has . . . And at his age . . .

FOX

That's the way.

GABRIEL

How the hell could she have picked up poison around here? For Christ's sake, no one sets poison in the middle of a bog!

FOX *shrugs his shoulders and moves away.* GABRIEL *glances at him, then looks at him, then stares.*

Fox . . .

FOX

(*Quickly, defensively*) Well?

GABRIEL

God, Fox . . . you didn't?

FOX

What are you mouthing about?

GABRIEL

You did?

FOX

Did what?

GABRIEL

Christ, man, how could you?

FOX

Who are you to talk?

GABRIEL

You might as well have killed Pedro himself.

FOX

It's a dog, remember—not an old woman.

GABRIEL

You did it . . . deliberately . . . to get rid of Pedro.

FOX

Shut up.

GABRIEL

Just as you got rid of the Fritter twins and Cid and Tanya
and all the others I heard about.

FOX

You know nothing about it.

GABRIEL

Why, man?

FOX

You know nothing about it.

GABRIEL

What are you at?

FOX

Just leave me. I'm managing fine.

GABRIEL

Fine? You call this fine? Wrecking the show? Killing an old man's dog? What are you doing?

Pause.

FOX

Once, maybe twice in your life, the fog lifts, and you get a glimpse, an intuition; and suddenly you know that this can't be all there is to it—there has to be something better than this.

GABRIEL

You're going mad! What fog?

FOX

And afterwards all you're left with is a vague memory of what you thought you saw; and that's what you hold on to—the good thing you think you saw.

GABRIEL

You planned it all! That's it. It's all deliberate!

FOX

Because there must be something better than this.

GABRIEL

It's some sort of a crazy scheme!

FOX

(*Wearily*) Go away, boy.

GABRIEL

You're full of hate—that's what's wrong with you—you hate everybody!

FOX

No.

GABRIEL

Even Crystal.

FOX

What about Crystal?

GABRIEL

She'll be the next. You'll ditch her too.

FOX

How little you know, boy. My Crystal is the only good part of me.

BRING DOWN LIGHTS

EPISODE 4

Night.

The stage is empty and almost totally dark.

Off right there are muffled sounds of excited voices. Then suddenly GABRIEL *enters right and races frantically across stage. He is in his bare feet, undervest, and trousers. As he gets to extreme left, a uniformed Irish* POLICEMAN *steps out of the shadows—and* GABRIEL *lands in his arms.*

POLICEMAN

The running's over. Take it easy, Melarkey.

Two plainclothes English DETECTIVES *enter right.*

DETECTIVE I

Hold him, Sergeant!

DETECTIVE 2

The bastard bit my hand! (*Produces handcuffs.*) Hold them out, Paddy. When I get you back, I'll fix your teeth.

GABRIEL *holds out his hands.* DETECTIVE 2 *hits him in the lower stomach.* GABRIEL *doubles up.*

POLICEMAN
No need for that.

DETECTIVE 2
And that's only the beginning, Paddy. A warming up, you might say.

POLICEMAN
Better get some clothes for him.

DETECTIVE 1
I'll get them.

POLICEMAN
And shoes.

DETECTIVE 1 *leaves.*

DETECTIVE 2
I'd take him as he is. (*Catches* GABRIEL *by the chin.*) Might cool you off, Paddy, eh? And I want you to know me. My name's Coalstream. Been after you for quite a while now, Paddy. And after I've finished with you, you'll be sorry you ever left your gypsy encampment.

POLICEMAN
You'll be charged in the station.

DETECTIVE 2

And in the morning we go to Manchester. By plane. For speed, Paddy. Extradition papers—reservations—all in order. You're quite a big piece of dirt; you know that, Paddy?

Enter FOX *and* CRYSTAL *wearing coats over their nightclothes.* FOX *is carrying a hurricane lamp.*

FOX

What the hell's all the—

CRYSTAL

Fox! It's Gabriel!

DETECTIVE 2

You two his parents?

CRYSTAL

What's wrong? Who are you? (*Sees handcuffs.*) Why is he handcuffed?

DETECTIVE 2

He's under arrest, missus. And tomorrow afternoon he'll be charged in Manchester with the manslaughter of an old lady two months ago.

CRYSTAL

Murder? . . . Gabriel?

DETECTIVE 2

He's lucky it's not murder.

CRYSTAL

Oh my God . . .

FOX *holds her arm to steady her.*

GABRIEL

He (FOX) knew. I told him.

CRYSTAL

It's lies! It's lies!

DETECTIVE 2

Why don't you ask him (GABRIEL), missus? He knows all about it.

CRYSTAL

Why didn't you tell me, Fox? Why didn't you tell me?

FOX

Easy, my love. Shhhh.

DETECTIVE I *returns with* GABRIEL's *shoes and clothes. Because he is handcuffed, the jacket is draped over his shoulders. The* POLICE- MAN *puts the shoes on his feet. While this is going on:*

CRYSTAL

Manchester? . . . Why are you taking him there?

DETECTIVE 1

That's where he coshed the old lady. Twenty-nine stitches she got. You've a boy to be proud of, missus—a real gentleman.

CRYSTAL

I'm going, too. Wherever you're taking him, I'm going too.

GABRIEL

I'll be all right, Crystal.

DETECTIVE 1

You can't hold his hand in jail for ten years.

DETECTIVE 2

He'll do. I've a special heater in the car for him.

CRYSTAL

Fox—!

FOX

Easy, easy, easy.

DETECTIVE 2

Bloody gypsies. Same all over.

FOX

Where are you taking him to?

POLICEMAN

To the station. Then to Dublin . . .

CRYSTAL

Stop them, Fox! Stop them!

DETECTIVE 1

He'll get a fair trial, missus.

DETECTIVE 2

He'll get his deserts. Come on.

CRYSTAL

Give him back to me!

She breaks away from FOX *and flings herself at the police. There is a brief scuffle. She is thrown to the ground.*

DETECTIVE 2

Stinking gypsies! Let's go.

The two detectives move off with GABRIEL *between them.* CRYSTAL *does not hear the following:*

POLICEMAN

I warned you to get out of my territory, Melarkey.

FOX

How did you know he was here?

POLICEMAN

The old man in hospital spilled the beans.

FOX

Papa?!

POLICEMAN

The old doting man. Everyone that lights in his ward, he asks them to tell Gabriel to come and see him.

FOX

And some rat went and told you?

POLICEMAN

He told me himself, Melarkey. And if the boy had gone to see him—even once—the old man would have been content and we might never have known. (*Leaves.*)

FOX *turns round, sees* CRYSTAL *sobbing. He sits beside her and puts his arms around her.*

CRYSTAL

Gabriel . . .

FOX

My love.

CRYSTAL

My boy.

FOX

It's all right . . . all right . . .

CRYSTAL

My Gabriel.

FOX

Easy . . . easy . . .

She sobs convulsively. FOX *holds her head to his shoulder.*

BRING DOWN LIGHTS

EPISODE 5

When the lights come up, dawn is breaking. FOX *and* CRYSTAL *are dressed as we left them.* CRYSTAL *is sitting on an upturned box, staring at the dead stove. They have not been in bed all night and their conversation has an exhausted and ragged inconsequence.*

FOX *has been watching the dawn break. He now moves over beside her.*

FOX

The sun's coming up. (*Sits beside her and takes her hand.*) My sweet?

CRYSTAL

My Fox.

FOX

How do you feel?

CRYSTAL

Not bad.

FOX

You should lie down for a while now.

CRYSTAL

You know I couldn't sleep.

FOX

(*Briskly, the entertainer*) That's what I'll do, then. This very morning. "Mr. Prospect," I'll say, "because of considerations of health, the Fox Melarkey Show is prepared to—to—to consider a take-over bid offered by you, provided, of course, the financial terms are acceptable to the joint shareholders of the Melarkey board." Eh? No—"provided the cash settlement is realistic in terms of our national reputation and all currently functioning equipment." How about that?

CRYSTAL

What's that, Fox?

FOX

Is that all right?

CRYSTAL

(*Listless*) That's good. That's fine.

FOX

Everything except the accordion and the rickety wheel.

CRYSTAL

And this (*stove*) too.

FOX

What d'you think his offer'll be?

CRYSTAL

Couldn't even make a guess, my pet.

FOX

Well, I mean to say, there's the truck; and two vans—one in semi-mint condition; and the marquee and the stage; and the ornate proscenium and velour curtains; and—and —and—and, of course, the reputation and good will—if he offers me sixty quid for the lot, Jaysus, I'll take the arm off him.

CRYSTAL

It's cold.

FOX

You're tired.

CRYSTAL

I'll get some solicitor to defend him, won't I?

FOX

Flash the money, my love, and you'll get the Lord Chief Justice.

CRYSTAL

I just can't get it out of my head . . . not Gabriel, some-how . . . he was never that kind . . . or maybe you never know anybody.

FOX

They'll be in Dublin by now.

CRYSTAL

If he'd been a rough boy or anything. But he's so . . . so soft . . . at least I thought he was.

FOX

Probably he panicked.

CRYSTAL

Those shoes (FOX's) are letting in.

FOX

The ground's dry.

CRYSTAL

"There's no worse shod than a shoemaker's wife"—that was a great expression of Papa's. I never knew what it meant.

FOX

I think we shouldn't tell him about Gabriel.

CRYSTAL

Makes no difference now. He's past understanding.

FOX

Maybe.

CRYSTAL

Sure you know he's completely doting.

FOX

I suppose so. (*Rises.*) A strange time of day, this . . . Every time I see the sun coming up, I think of the morning we—(*He breaks off and looks at her.*) Do you remember the channel?

CRYSTAL

What's that?

He begins quietly, diffidently. But as he recalls the episode—and as she remembers it, too—his warmth and obvious joy spread to her.

FOX

A few miles north of Galway—along the coast—a channel of water—a stream—just where it entered the sea. We were only two weeks married at the time.

CRYSTAL

(*Listlessly*) Galway's nice.

FOX

(*Sitting beside her*) And you got a mad notion of going for a swim at dawn. And this morning, just about this time, you woke me up, and we slipped out and raced across the wet fields in our bare feet. And when we got to the sea, we had to wade across this stream to get to the beach.

CRYSTAL

(*Suddenly remembering.*) The channel!

FOX

D'you remember? And you hoisted up your skirt and you took my hand and we stepped into the—

CRYSTAL

Fish! Flat fish!

FOX

Hundreds of them! Every step you took! D'you remember?

CRYSTAL

Oh my God!

FOX

Every time you put a foot down!

CRYSTAL

The wriggling of them! Under your bare feet!

FOX

And you couldn't go forward! And you couldn't go back!

CRYSTAL

And you splitting your sides laughing!

FOX

Trying to keep hopping so that you wouldn't touch bottom!

CRYSTAL

Squirming and wriggling!

FOX

And then you lost your balance—and down you went!

CRYSTAL

And pulled you down, too.

FOX

And then you started to laugh!

CRYSTAL

It was the sight of you spluttering!

FOX

The water was freezing!

CRYSTAL

We were soaked to the skin!

FOX

And we staggered over to the beach.

CRYSTAL

And you, you eejit, you began to leap about like a monkey!

FOX

The seagulls—remember?—they sat on the rocks, staring at us.

CRYSTAL

And you tied a plait of seaweed to my hair.

FOX

And we danced on the sand.

CRYSTAL

Wet clothes and all.

FOX

And then the sun came out.

CRYSTAL

The channel . . . Funny, I'd forgotten that altogether.

FOX

Just the two of us.

Silence: each with his own thoughts.

CRYSTAL

Fox, I was thinking—

FOX

(*Eagerly*) What?

CRYSTAL

Before you had this idea of selling out, I was thinking where we could raise the money for a solicitor.

FOX

(*Flatly*) Oh.

CRYSTAL

And Pedro was the only person I could think of. He offered me money before, you know.

FOX

A good man.

CRYSTAL

A great man. I wonder where he's disappeared to?

FOX

God knows.

CRYSTAL

He used to talk to that dog as if it was a baby.

FOX

That's the way.

CRYSTAL

Maybe he went to Dublin; he has a cousin there.

FOX

She died years ago.

CRYSTAL

I didn't know that. How long does it take to fly from Dublin to Manchester?

FOX

About an hour.

CRYSTAL

I don't think he was ever in an airplane before, was he?

FOX

Not that I know of.

FOX *is conscious that he should match* CRYSTAL'*s somber mood. But he is unable to suppress the strange excitement he feels. He moves closer to her.*

My sweet—

CRYSTAL

My Fox.

FOX

My sweet, when we get rid of this stuff to Prospect—

CRYSTAL

Maybe he won't touch it.

FOX

Don't you worry: I'll get rid of it. And when I do there'll just be you and me and the old accordion and the old rickety wheel—all we had thirty years ago, remember? You and me. And we'll laugh again at silly things and I'll plait seaweed into your hair again. And we'll go only to the fairs we want to go to, and stop only at the towns we want to stop at, and eat when we want to eat, and lie down when we feel like it. And everywhere we go, we'll know people and they'll know us—"Crystal and Fox!" Jaysus, my love, if I weren't a superstitious man, I'd say— I'd say—

CRYSTAL

What?

FOX

I'd say that heaven's just round the corner.

BRING DOWN LIGHTS

EPISODE 6

Two days later.

A crossroads in the open country. A signpost pointing in four directions. It is a beautiful sunny day.

From some distance off can be heard the sound of FOX *and* CRYSTAL *approaching. They make so much noise—chattering, laughing, whooping, singing—that one would expect to see a dozen happy children appear.*

Now they arrive at the crossroads. FOX *is carrying the rickety wheel, the accordion, and the stove.* CRYSTAL *is carrying two shabby suitcases.* FOX *has a bottle of wine in his pocket, and when their hands are free, the bottle passes between them. Neither is drunk, or even tipsy, but both are more than a little elated: all their immediate worries have been solved; and the afternoon is warm; and the wine is heady.* FOX *is particularly jaunty and vivacious, like a young man being flamboyant to entertain and impress his girl.*

FOX

This is it! Here we are!

CRYSTAL

Where?

FOX

Here!

CRYSTAL

You're pulling my leg!

FOX

Anything that's going anywhere has to pass here. Dublin—
Galway—Cork—Derry; you're at the hub of the country,
girl.

CRYSTAL

The hub of the country! Fox, you're an eejit!

FOX

(*Sings*) "A-hitching we will go / A-hitching we will go!"
Throw your stuff down there and leave everything to the
Fox. Two single tickets to—where do you wish to go to,
madam?

CRYSTAL

Manchester!

FOX

Manchester it'll be!

CRYSTAL *drops down on the side of the road.*

CRYSTAL

(*Giggling*) No one's ever going to stop, my Fox. They're all going to swizzzzz right past. And we're going to spend the rest of our lives in the middle of nowhere. God, I'm giddy!

FOX

(*Toasting*) To a great day's work. To your lawyer, Mr. King—

CRYSTAL

Ring! Frederick Ashley Ring!

FOX

—who'll see that our boy is well defended; and to Dick Prospect, who parted with forty crisp notes for a load of rubbish and for a truck that won't go into reverse.

CRYSTAL

You didn't tell him?!

FOX

D'you think I'm mad? He kept saying, "She runs sweet enough, Fox, I can see that. Turn her at this gate and take me back." "No, no, Dick, a fair trial; we'll go right round the circuit. I want you to know what you're getting."

CRYSTAL

Too damn good for him!

FOX

And when we got back to his place, who d'you think I saw?

CRYSTAL

Who?

FOX

Cid.

CRYSTAL

You did not!

FOX

Eating a big feed of bacon and eggs—his van door was open; and she was standing outside, screaming in at him.

CRYSTAL

What about?

FOX

"You've lost control! And don't blame me if your stomach curdles and gripes on you!"

CRYSTAL *rolls over with laughter.*

This is the life, girl; it should always have been like this. (*He hears a car approaching.*) Transport! Transport! We're in business! This is it. We're away! Gather up your things! (*He hides the bottle, straightens his tie, assumes a pleasant face, does a brief jig for* CRYSTAL's *entertainment, and takes up his position at the verge of the road.*)

CRYSTAL

God, this is a scream!

FOX

(*To car*) Come on, come on—that's it, me aul darlin'—a lift for the Crystal and the Fox—slow down—that's it—decent fella—we'll go wherever you're going—look at the wee narrow shoulders and the wee sad face smiling in at you—

CRYSTAL

(*Laughing*) You eejit, you!

FOX

—sure you never saw anything as pathetic in all your life—the honest Fox Melarkey depending on charity for his transportation and edification—

CRYSTAL

(*Laughing*) Quit it, Fox!

FOX

Doesn't hear a word I'm saying. (*To car*) May God reward you for your years of dedication to our little mission hospital here in Lakula in Eastern Tipperary—Jaysus, you couldn't say no to a pair of innocent eyes like these—Jaysus, you could—Jaysus, you're a hoor!

The car has gone past. Peals of laughter from CRYSTAL.

(*To car*) And in the next bad frost I hope they drop off you!

CRYSTAL

He heard you, you clown, you!

FOX *is moved by a strange elation: not so much joy as a controlled recklessness. The sun, the wine, the release from responsibility, the desire to play up to an easy audience like* CRYSTAL—*these are all the obvious ingredients of his exultation. But he is aware—and* CRYSTAL *is not—that it has also a cold, brittle quality, an edge of menace. He gives the rickety wheel a sharp turn, and addresses an imaginary crowd:*

FOX

Red, yellow, black, or blue, whatever it is that tickles your fancy, now's your chance to turn a bad penny into a decent pound, there's a wee lassie out there that looks as if she might, come on, my love, now's your chance, if you wait till your mother tells you, the notion'll have gone off you.

CRYSTAL

Take a swig before it's done.

FOX

No more for me.

CRYSTAL

All the better.

FOX

(*Irritably*) Are there no bloody cars in the country?

CRYSTAL

Lie back here beside me and relax.

FOX

I have to be on the move. (*Eagerly*) My Crystal, let's get married again!

CRYSTAL

You're drunk.

FOX

My love, marry me again. Please marry me again.

CRYSTAL

Full as a pig!

FOX

I'm asking you, my sweet.

CRYSTAL

Here?

FOX

Now.

CRYSTAL

At this moment?

FOX

Immediately.

CRYSTAL

In these clothes?

FOX

Just as you are.

CRYSTAL

This is so sudden. But why not? You only die once! (*Rises and sings*) "Here comes the bride, small, fat, and wide—" (*She breaks off suddenly.*) A car!

FOX

(*Irritably*) Let it pass.

CRYSTAL

A big swanky one! Come on, Fox; do your job!

FOX

I hear no car.

CRYSTAL

There it is. Quick! Hide that bottle!

FOX

(*Vaguely*) Will I try it?

CRYSTAL

What d'you mean—will you try it? You don't want to be stuck in this godforsaken place, do you? Will you try it! What's wrong with you, man?

FOX

(*Very sharply*) Okay. Okay. Stop nagging!

CRYSTAL

"Will I try it!"

He faces the approaching car and switches on his professional smile.

FOX

That's it—take it easy—slow now—slower—

CRYSTAL

We're away this time!

FOX

Good day to you, ma'am—Fox and Crystal, a professional couple temporarily inconvenienced and maladjusted—Me-

larkey's the name—and who's to say, perhaps the first lay
Pope—

CRYSTAL

Ha-ha-ha-ha!

FOX

That'll be an entry for your diary: "Today I gave a lift to
the Supreme Pontiff and his missus, outside the village of
Slaughmanus"—

CRYSTAL

She hears you, you fool, you!

FOX

Wait—wait—wait—wait—

The car has gone.

CRYSTAL

She heard every word you said!

FOX

(*Shouts*) With a face like that, you'd need a Rolls! Ele-
phant!

CRYSTAL

That sun's roasting.

FOX

We've got to move. We must keep moving.

CRYSTAL

Honest to God, my sweet, I'm tipsy! Haven't seen Dickie Prospect for years. How's he looking?

FOX

As usual.

CRYSTAL

Was he asking for Crystal?

FOX

You're plastered.

CRYSTAL

Don't tell me my Fox is jealous!

FOX

Of that animal? Jaysus!

CRYSTAL

Don't worry, my sweet. It was a long, long, long time ago, before I met my Fox.

FOX

Animal.

CRYSTAL

And he never, never, never crosses my mind.

FOX

What the hell sort of a dead end is this?

CRYSTAL

Very pretty. And the sun's warm. And there's a smell of heather. And I feel . . . gorgeous. D'you think I'm gorgeous, my pet?

No response from FOX.

My Fox.

FOX

Mm?

CRYSTAL

Sit down here beside me.

FOX

Can't sit.

CRYSTAL

We're all rotten, my sweet.

FOX

You're drunk.

CRYSTAL

I am not drunk, Fox. But I am rotten. Papa's dying in hospital. Gabriel's going to jail. The show's finished. We've no money. And I'm happy as a lark. Amn't I rotten, my Fox?

He does not answer.

Fox.

FOX

Maybe we should try the other road.

CRYSTAL

You changed, my pet.

FOX

Or go back to the village.

CRYSTAL

You think I didn't notice. But I did. Crystal saw it all.

FOX

Good for Crystal.

CRYSTAL

Just when things were beginning to go well for the show, too. And then you got . . . restless. That's what happened. My Fox got restless. Out go the Fritter twins. Out goes Billy Hercules. And I was frightened, 'cos I thought:

he's going to wreck it all, break it all up. That's when it began. Am I right, my sweet?

FOX

You shouldn't drink, woman.

CRYSTAL

And then you began to skip the places that were good in the past. And when we could have done four nights, you left after two. And then you poisoned Pedro's dog—

FOX

You don't know what you're saying!

CRYSTAL

You did, my love. I know you did. And I never understood why you did those things. I wondered, of course, 'cos I know you loved him. But I never understood. And maybe I didn't want to know, my Fox, because I was afraid—it was the only fear I had—I was terrified that you were going to shake me off too. And I really didn't give a damn about any of them, God forgive me, not even Pedro, not as long as you didn't turn on me. That's all I cared about. And now we're back at the start, my love; just as we began together. Fox and Crystal. To hell with everything else.

This revelation stuns FOX. *He stares at her in utter amazement and incredulity.*

FOX

And Pedro?

CRYSTAL

Crystal saw it all.

FOX

You knew?

CRYSTAL

I told you—I'm rotten.

FOX

That I had killed the one good thing he had?

CRYSTAL

God forgive me, Fox.

FOX

Our friend, Pedro?

CRYSTAL

What are you looking at me like that for? It was you that did it, remember; not me. Here, my love, sit down here beside me.

As if he were in a dream, he goes to her and sits beside her. She catches his hand.

I'd marry you a dozen—a hundred times again.

FOX

Would you?

CRYSTAL

Every day. Every hour. (*She closes her eyes and rests her head on his shoulder.*) My sweet Fox . . . This is all I want.

When FOX *speaks, his voice is very soft, almost comforting.* CRYSTAL's *replies are sun-drowsy.*

FOX

My pet . . .

CRYSTAL

Mm?

FOX

You love me, Crystal.

CRYSTAL

Mm.

FOX

You love me, don't you?

CRYSTAL

Sweet Fox.

FOX

A lot—a great lot?

CRYSTAL

Mm.

FOX

(*More slowly*) If you were asked to, would you go to hell with me?

CRYSTAL

There and back, my love.

Pause.

FOX

Crystal.

CRYSTAL

Can't keep awake.

FOX

I have something to tell you.

CRYSTAL

Tell me.

FOX

About Gabriel.

CRYSTAL

He was always such a gentle boy.

FOX

You don't know how they found him.

CRYSTAL

Who, my pet?

FOX

How the police found him.

CRYSTAL

What d'you mean, my Fox?

FOX

Do you remember that night he came—just after Cid and Tanya had gone—remember that night?

CRYSTAL

Yes.

FOX

Well, he told me the whole story that night—about what happened, and how he hid in Glasgow and then slipped over on the boat.

CRYSTAL

I know.

FOX

And then he told me about the reward.

CRYSTAL

The what?

FOX

The English police offered a reward of £100 for him: or £50 for any information about him.

CRYSTAL *sits up*.

I did nothing for a while, couldn't make up my mind. And then one day when we were passing through Ballymore, I went into the police station there, the white building at the end of the town, and the motorcycle policeman—remember him?—he was there, and I—I—I told him that Gabriel was traveling with us.

CRYSTAL *rises*.

CRYSTAL

You?

FOX

So they asked me a few questions. And then they made me wait until they phoned Dublin. And Dublin phoned Manchester. And that was it. That's how he was caught.

CRYSTAL

Fox . . . ?

FOX

So whenever we get to Dublin next, there's £100 waiting there for us.

CRYSTAL

You're lying—

FOX

I don't think Gabriel knows; they probably didn't tell him.

CRYSTAL

You're lying, Fox!—you're lying—lying! (*She leaps at him, catches his shirt, and puts her face into his.*) Jesus, man, deny it!

FOX

It's the truth.

CRYSTAL

It's a lie! Not your own son! Not Gabriel!

FOX

We need the money. It'll start us off again.

She lets him go, staring at him.

CRYSTAL

Your own son? . . . To the police? . . .

FOX

It's a lot of money.

CRYSTAL *steps back from him.*

CRYSTAL

What . . . are . . . you? (*He puts out a hand to touch her. She recoils and screams.*) Don't—don't—don't touch me! (*She backs away from him.*) Get away from me! Don't come near me! Don't touch me! Don't speak to me! Don't even look at me! Must get away from you— evil . . . a bad man . . . It's too much . . . I don't know you . . . Don't know you at all . . . Never knew . . . never . . . (*She breaks away from him in a frenzy. She lifts her coat and a case, all the time sobbing and mumbling incoherently. We hear: "Gabriel . . . Never—never . . . Pedro . . . My boy . . . Evil . . ."*)

FOX

I needn't have told you. You need never have known.

She has her belongings. She hesitates and looks at him with total bewilderment.

CRYSTAL

I don't know who you are. (*Runs off.*)

FOX *takes a few steps after her.*

FOX

Crystal! (*Loudly*) Crystal! (*Quietly, tensely*) It's a lie, Crystal, all a lie, my love, I made it all up, never entered my head until a few minutes ago and then I tried to stop myself but I couldn't, it was poor Papa that told the police and he didn't know what he was saying, I don't know why I said it, I said it just to—to—to—(*Roars*) Crystal! (*Again quiet, rapid*) Lies, lies, yes, I wanted rid of the Fritters and Billy Hercules, yes, I wanted rid of Cid and Tanya, and I wanted rid of the whole show, everything, even good Pedro, because that's what I saw, that's the glimpse I got for the moment the fog lifted, that's what I remember, that's what I think I remember, just you and me as we were, but we were young then, and even though our clothes were wet and even though the sun was only rising, there were hopes—there were warm hopes; and love alone isn't enough now, my Crystal, it's not, my love, not enough at all, not nearly enough. (*Viciously turns the rickety wheel.*) Red, yellow, black, or blue, whatever it is that tickles your fancy, now's your chance to turn a bad penny into a decent pound, I love you, my Crystal, and you are the best part of me, and I don't know where I'm going or what will become of me, I might have stumbled on as I did once, but I got an inkling, my Crystal, and I had to hold on to that; Crystal, my Crystal, where am I now, my Crystal? (*Turns the rickety wheel listlessly and sings lamely*.) "A-hunting you will go / A-hunting you will go / You'll catch no fox and put him in a box / A-hunting you will go." (*Fairground voice*) Red, yellow, black, or blue, whatever it is that tickles your fancy, the Fox knows all the answers—what it's all about, that's why he's dressed in velvets and drives about in a swank car, you're looking straight at the man that sleeps content at night because he's learned the secrets of the universe, strike me dead if I'm telling a lie and you wipe that grin off your jaw, lady, when you're at a wake, red, yellow, black, or blue, you pays your money and you takes your choice, not that it makes a damn bit of difference, because the whole thing's fixed, my love, fixed—fixed—fixed . . . (*Almost gently*) But who am I to cloud your bright eyes or kill your belief that love is all. A penny a time and you think you'll be happy for life.

A car passes. He does not hear it. He closes his eyes, puts his arm over the rickety wheel, and quickly buries his face in his arm.

CURTAIN

Crystal and Fox was first performed at the Gaiety Theatre, Dublin, on Tuesday, November 12, 1968. It was directed by Hilton Edwards, with the following cast:

Fox Melarkey	CYRIL CUSACK
Crystal Melarkey	MAUREEN TOAL
Papa	JOHN MCDARBY
Pedro	CECIL SHERIDAN
El Cid	ROBERT CARRICKFORD
Tanya	YVONNE COOPER
Gabriel	CHRIS O'NEILL
Irish Policeman	NIALL O'BRIAIN
English Detective	BRENDAL SULLIVAN
English Detective	TOM IRVINE

The Mundy Scheme

OR, MAY WE WRITE YOUR EPITAPH NOW, MR. EMMET?

Characters

ROGER NASH, *private secretary to the Taoiseach (Prime Minister)*
SALLY, *typist-receptionist*
F. X. RYAN, *Taoiseach*
NEIL BOYLE, *Minister for Finance*
MRS. RYAN, *Taoiseach's mother*
MICHAEL MOLONEY, *Minister for External Affairs*
DAN MAHON, *Minister for Development*
CHARLES HOGAN, *Minister for Commerce*
(MISS) PAT TOYE, *TV producer*
SEAN O'GRADY, *TV cameraman*
TONY HANLAN, *TV lighting man*
OWEN, *TV sound man*
PRELUDE ANNOUNCER

The Set

Because he is house-bound, F. X. RYAN has converted his drawing room—a large, spacious, well-proportioned room—into an office. The conversion has been a failure: the room is now a mess, neither comfortable nor efficient.

His immense mahogany desk, stage left, and facing across stage, is cluttered with papers, reports, documents, two phones, and an intercom.

Below the desk is a television set facing up-stage.

There are two windows on the back wall, both curtained with faded and sagging green velour. Between them is a large, framed map of Ireland. Below them is a couch.

His private secretary's desk is stage right, facing the Taoiseach's. It is smaller and perfectly organized: precise piles of letters, papers, documents, a portable typewriter carefully in its cover, today's newspapers neatly stacked, a phone.

A few occasional chairs, remnants of a dining-room suite. An occasional table, on which sits a vase of limp roses. A wall safe behind RYAN's desk.

A huge chandelier hangs from the ceiling.

A door, stage right, leads to the typist/reception room. A door, stage left, leads to the living quarters.

The place is Dublin. The time is at hand.

ACT ONE

When the curtain rises, ROGER NASH *is dictating letters to* SALLY (*miming until the voice has finshed the Prelude*). NASH *is a personable young man in his late twenties: cool, calm, precise, efficient—qualities that in his work compensate for his real obtuseness and adequately conceal his absorbing bitterness. He dictates quickly and mechanically and in a voice that hints at his distaste for the people he is writing to. He speaks official jargon fluently. When he finishes one letter, he drops it into the wastepaper basket at his feet and goes on to the next almost without halting. Everything he does is unrushed and well oiled.*

The Prelude is spoken in a cultured accent.

VOICE

Ladies and gentlemen: What happens when a small nation that has been manipulated and abused by a huge colonial power for hundreds of years wrests its freedom by blood and anguish? What happens to an emerging country after it has emerged? Does the transition from dependence to independence induce a fatigue, a mediocrity, an ennui? Or does the clean spirit of idealism that fired the people to freedom augment itself, grow bolder, more revolutionary, more generous?

The answer to many of these questions can be found in Ireland, a little island in the Atlantic Ocean, 350 miles long, 150 miles broad, and with a population of about four million people. For seven hundred years this little island was occupied and oppressed by the English, who treated the natives as serfs and who even tried to supplant the Catholic religion, which was beloved by the natives, by the Protestant faith, which—which wasn't really suited to the moist and temperate climate. Many times the people rose up against their overlords but each time they were beaten down and reduced to even greater serfdom. Eventually, however, in the year 1916, led by a handful of idealists they rose again and this time they overthrew the English.

After their rebellion, it was a strange experience for these hardy island people to find themselves their own masters; and they were so confused that for a time they squabbled among themselves. But they soon realized that they had better put their little green isle in order if they hoped to create the nation that the idealists of 1916 would have been proud of. So they set to with a new vigor. And the results of their endeavors are something like this . . .

Ladies and gentlemen: The Mundy Scheme; or May We Write Your Epitaph Now, Mr. Emmet?

NASH

. . . we should certainly like to, but taking all these elements into consideration and in view of the fact that the economy of the country is currently . . . less resilient than one would wish, the Taoiseach asks me to inform you that at the moment he cannot support in principle the channeling of any state monies whatever into any new industry. He wishes you to understand, however, that when the present situation is relieved, the government will give sympathetic attention to any reasonable proposal. (*Phone rings.*) Sincerely, Roger Nash, private secretary to the Taoiseach. I'll take it. Hello, good morning, Mr. Boyle . . . No, I'm sorry, he hasn't appeared yet . . . Certainly I'll tell him . . . Oh, he's feeling much better now, much . . . Thank you, sir. Goodbye. (*Hangs up.*) Boyle's back from Zurich. Doesn't sound too happy. Any more official stuff?

SALLY

That's the last, Mr. Nash.

NASH

Let's wade into the rubbish, then.

SALLY

Mr. Nash, would you mind if I slipped across the street to get a packet of cigarettes? I'd only be a—

NASH

Sorry. Miss Bridie Towers, 27 Glenview, Limerick. Dear Miss Towers: The Taoiseach is grateful for your message of good will for his speedy recovery. You will be pleased to learn that Mr. Ryan hopes to be well enough to resume work in the near future. Sincerely, Roger Nash, et cetera, et cetera. Miss Evelyn Smyth—with a "y"—The Old Rectory, Ballymore. Dear Miss Smyth: the Taoiseach values your suggestions for the disposal of nuclear waste and will bear them in mind . . . when the situation arises. (*Phone.*) Sincerely, et cetera. Hello . . . No, your Grace, this is his secretary . . . Nothing serious, your Grace, just a recurrence of his old trouble, labyrinthitis. If it weren't for the sudden bouts of dizziness and nausea, he could be out and—very embarrassing, your Grace, that's why we have transferred his office to his home here . . . Indeed I will . . . Very kind of you, your Grace; 7:30 tomorrow morning; very grateful; thank you very much . . . Goodbye. (*Hangs up.*) Where was I? Yes, Mr. Sean Quin, County Councillor, Kelly's Corner, County Mayo. Quin —he's one of the old brigade. Better make this first-person —in the vernacular. Dear Sean: How's the big heart? My God but it's bloody powerful to hear from you, even though you're complaining as usual, and aul hoor—a-u-l w-h-o-r-e. Of course I'm worried about the high emigration from your area and from the whole west. But I promise you, Sean a Vic, that I have the situation under constant survey. Love to my old sweetheart, Flo—

SALLY

A-u-l?

NASH

What?

SALLY

A-u-l sweetheart Flo?

NASH

O-l-d. Sweetheart, Flo, and to all the kiddies. Affection-
ately, F. X. Ryan—no, just F.X. Is that the lot?

SALLY

Just an anonymous one.

NASH

". . . your whole party is crooked but Moloney, the Minister for External Affairs, and you, Ryan, is the biggest
gangsters of them all. Why don't the two of you . . ."
Tch-tch-tch.

SALLY

There's some signature.

NASH

"Disgusted" . . . Probably the leader of the opposition.
Nothing else?

SALLY

This one about the house in County Meath.

NASH

Here it is. To Mrs. Mary Kerr of—

SALLY

I have the address.

NASH

Dear Madam: Since he became Taoiseach, Mr. F. X. Ryan has not practiced as an auctioneer. I suggest, however, that you entrust the sale of your property to his nephew, Mr. Declan Ryan, Ballybeg, who is presently conducting the firm's affairs. Sincerely. And that's it. What about his article for the *Industrial Review*? He'll want to read it before it goes off.

SALLY

On his desk, typed and ready.

Enter FRANCIS XAVIER RYAN, *wearing a smoking jacket and slippers. He is fifty, but looks younger. Physically very strong, with blunt, regular features and alert eyes. He has never been ill in his life, and is alternately petulant and aggressive at this bout of labyrinthitis, partly because it has confined him to the house, but more because it strikes him as grossly unfair. He is a bachelor.*

If he were to philosophize about his work, he would certainly conclude that politics is a natural extension of the auctioneering business. His mind is quick and enormously cunning. With no effort at all he can assume anger, frustration, delight, simplicity, honesty, fury, and a dozen other faces: and once he has put on a particular face, his emotions invariably and obligingly support it so that he is never conscious of putting on a performance. He has no illusions about other people and only one pardonable illusion about himself: he believes that he is a patriot. He is secretly devoted to his mother.

RYAN

Morning, Sally. Morning, Roger.

SALLY

Good morning, Mr. Ryan.

NASH

How do you feel today?

RYAN

Rotten. Any word from Moloney?

NASH

Nothing, sir.

RYAN

My God, he's a bloody hoor, that fella. (*To* SALLY, *as she exits*) Sally, get me New York.

NASH

I rang them an hour ago.

RYAN

Well?

NASH

There hasn't been a meeting of the Central Assembly for four days and they thought at the embassy that he was back here.

SALLY

I rang his home. Mrs. Moloney hasn't seen him since last Friday.

RYAN

If he's on the bottle, I'll personally break his bloody neck. (*To* SALLY) All right. Try London. And if he's not there, try Paris. And if he's not there . . . go and pull him out of O'Donnell's bar.

SALLY *leaves.* RYAN *sits behind his desk and covers his face with his hands.*

Republic on brink of collapse. Minister for External Affairs vanishes. Right, Roger, feed me the good news of the day with your usual discretion.

NASH

It's pretty bad, Mr. Ryan.

RYAN

It can only be bad if you expect something.

NASH

Well, sir . . . (*Plunging in*) The strike is twelve weeks old today, and as from next Monday all petrol and oil reserves will be exhausted and the country'll be at a complete halt.

RYAN

Good.

NASH

Provisional export figures for the last quarter are just out: lowest in eight years.

RYAN

Good.

NASH

The opposition are seeing the President tomorrow to demand your resignation, the dissolution of the Dail, and the setting up of a commission to run the country for at least two years.

RYAN

Fine.

NASH

Flour supplies are dwindling rapidly and Curley McMurray says his unions won't allow an airlift.

RYAN

Great.

NASH

The Minister for Finance is just back from Zurich.

RYAN

What's that?

NASH

Mr. Boyle, he rang, he's coming straight over.

RYAN

Well?

NASH

He indicated nothing to me, sir.

RYAN

How did he sound?

NASH

Restrained.

RYAN

Go on.

NASH

The Minister for Development wants to see you as soon—

RYAN

I'm seeing nobody until I've seen Boyle. What about the papers?

NASH

Predictable. Ours says we're on the threshold of a great new era; theirs says we're on the point of national death; and *The Times* pleads for a period of calm and reflection. You've been made a life patron of the Auctioneers' Alliance; I canceled your speech at the insurance dinner; and the U. S. Naval Attaché in London requests another meeting.

RYAN

I told him no last month.

NASH

I've arranged it tentatively for the fourteenth.

RYAN

What's that?

NASH

That's rather amusing. A poll by *Paris-Match* for the world's most eligible bachelor—you come twenty-seventh. And this is your article for the *Industrial Review*.

RYAN *leafs through it.*

What else is there? Yes, a request from the Zambian government for permission to send two delegates to study the workings of our Arts Council.

RYAN

Arts Council? I thought we scrapped that under Emergency Requisitions?

NASH

No, sir. We only cut off all subsidies. The Minister for Defense is representing the government at Deputy Broderick's funeral this afternoon. The Chinese navy is having exercises off the Philippines and your mother is having—

RYAN

I know—I know.

NASH

She tried to evict Sally and me this morning.

RYAN

What d'you mean?

NASH

She thinks we're squatters.

RYAN

Was she . . . violent?

NASH

In language, sir.

RYAN

I'm sorry, Roger. I'll speak to her again. Having us all here has upset her routine. (*Referring to article*) For God's sake, I said that last month in Sligo!

NASH

What's that?

RYAN

"When I want to know what Ireland is thinking, I go to a secluded spot and look into my heart."

NASH

Yeats used that in—

RYAN

To hell with Yeats. People will think I spend my time upside down in the middle of a bloody bog.

Buzzer. NASH *answers it.*

And all this crap: ". . . a truly Christian society . . . the
Eight Beatitudes . . ." That was our campaign two elec-
tions back!

NASH

The Minister for External Affairs isn't in London or Paris.

RYAN

(*Into intercom*) Try Geneva. And if he isn't there, I'll
put an SOS out for the bastard. (*To* NASH) Ask the old
doll to make us coffee. (*Into intercom*) Get me William
Carrigan at Finance.

RYAN *takes pills from his pocket, swallows three, and washes them
down with water. When the phone rings, he answers it with ex-
cessive geniality.*

Bill? F.X. here. How's the big heart, Bill, eh? Fine,
thanks, Bill, fine, apart from—ha-ha-ha—apart from the
head staggers. And how's all your care? Anne and the
kids well? . . . Great, great. Look, Bill, about these provisional export figures, I was wondering would it be possible to—to—just to sit on them for twenty-four hours until . . . I know, Bill, I know. But Boyle's over in Zurich
and he's on the point of pulling off something pretty big
and if we were to foul his pitch with *provisional* figures
just at this moment . . . (*Sharply*) Yes, of course I do
. . . They're already gone? . . . (*Flatly*) All right, Bill,
all right, forget it. Doesn't matter. (*He hangs up.*)

SALLY *at door.*

SALLY

The Minister for Finance is here.

RYAN

(*Shouts*) Come on in, Neil. (*To* SALLY) See that we're not interrupted.

NEIL BOYLE *enters. Black hat, black top coat, black suit. Umbrella, briefcase. He is a frail, gray-faced, anxious, middle-aged man who looks as if he were about to succumb to exhaustion. Although his clothes are expensive and always immaculate, he looks more like a piano tuner than a Cabinet Minister.*

He speaks softly and with a slightly English accent: he was educated by the Jesuits. He would like to be Minister of Culture, if such a post existed.

He knows that his robust colleagues can—and usually do—shout him down, and his defense is a kind of monkish withdrawal: eyes down, hands folded, head to the side, resignation in the face of ignorance.

RYAN *rises to greet him enthusiastically.*

RYAN

Good to see you, Neil. How's the big heart?

BOYLE

You're on your feet again, F.X.?

They shake hands.

RYAN

Just about. How are you?

BOYLE

Tired.

RYAN

When did you get in?

BOYLE

Half an hour ago. Haven't been home yet. But I've seen the headlines.

RYAN

And they're not exaggerating. We're really on our knees this time. (*Eagerly*) Well, how was Zurich?

BOYLE

You're looking fine. Trouble with the ear again?

RYAN

The usual. But I'm over the worst now. Well? (BOYLE *shrugs*.) What does that mean?

BOYLE

Bad.

RYAN

How bad?

BOYLE

Couldn't be worse.

RYAN

No backing?

BOYLE

Not a cent.

RYAN

You said on the phone that—

BOYLE

That there was a measure of sympathy. In other words, they listened patiently to me. They'll listen to you all day. But after you've talked your toque thick, they say, "Collateral, Mr. Boyle, collateral." As Kingsforth of the British Treasury says, it's the only English word they pronounce correctly.

RYAN

Was he there too?

BOYLE

He has bought an apartment there.

RYAN

But didn't you point out to them that—?

BOYLE

That the Fourth Economic Programme is in chaos? That we haven't paid even the interest on their last two loans? Look, F.X., you can tell these people nothing that they don't already know about us. They even had the provisional trade figures before you had them. They were able to tell me all the details of Curley McMurray and the strikers taking over the post office—and doling out children's allowances to unmarried mothers first. They know about the three by-elections coming up and that we're going to lose all three. They know about the collapse of the Prefabricated Housing Scheme and the mutiny on the corvette.

RYAN

The big new Japanese plastic factory in Kilkenny.

BOYLE

They know about it. They own it.

RYAN

The fish-meal factory at Malin Head.

BOYLE

F.X., these men control the treasuries of at least five countries. They have shored us up twice already. And to put it crudely, they now think we're beyond repair.

RYAN

Beyond . . . ! Christ Al . . . !

BOYLE

And they're right—unless we take the only course that's open to us—

RYAN

I refuse to devalue again. England won't let me.

BOYLE

—accept the offer of the U.S. Defense Department.

RYAN

We've discussed and rejected that weeks—

BOYLE

Facilities for their nuclear subs in Cork and Galway—that's all they want. And I promise you, F.X.—and I have this from the Assistant Secretary of State himself—I promise you they'll not stand by and watch us fall asunder.

RYAN

No.

BOYLE

One will do, then. Let them have Galway. They'll settle for one.

RYAN

No.

BOYLE

For the use of one small port and the setting up of a tiny communications center, have you any idea what the benefits could be?

RYAN

Never.

BOYLE

A flood of capital investment into the country; an instant drop in emigration; full employment in a depressed area; a new airstrip capable of carrying the biggest jets—

RYAN

They really have you in their pockets, Neil.

BOYLE

I resent that, F.X.

RYAN

You really believe they make naïve deals like that? Just let us tie up in Cork or Galway or whatever and we'll take care of all your troubles?

BOYLE

International agreements are subject to—

RYAN

No, no, no! You can't be as green as that, Neil. And even if they were to give us all the riches of the world in exchange for a couple of ports—which I just don't believe— my answer would still be no.

BOYLE

Beggars can't be choosers.

RYAN

They can. Indeed they can. A beggar may be destitute but he can still have his honor and his integrity and his inde-

pendence. Whatever small strength we have is in our ab-
solute neutrality. Whatever small dignity we have is in
keeping clear of the East-West power struggle. But throw
open our doors to the American forces and we become
another kept woman and every other tiny independent
nation and every struggling emerging country would
spurn us—and rightly so. Isn't this true?

BOYLE *spreads his hands.*

Anyhow, Galway and Cork could only take subs of less
than 2,000 tons. Have a drink.

BOYLE
Thanks. (BOYLE *pours himself a drink. Silence.*) So what
now?

RYAN
Go back to Zurich.

BOYLE
Futile.

RYAN
One more try.

BOYLE
They're so polite and so interested—it's humiliating, F.X.
They sound as if they're sad that we're collapsing and that

we've lost the confidence of the people. They even expressed concern about your health.

RYAN

(*Siffens. With dignity*) What exactly does that mean?

BOYLE

That they think we'll be out of office within a month.

RYAN

I'm talking about my health—you said they expressed concern.

BOYLE

That's how well they're informed.

RYAN

What precisely was said?

BOYLE

It's irrelevant, F.X.—I don't remember—but it just shows you—

RYAN

Who expressed concern?

BOYLE

I really don't remember, F.X. It was an aside. Maybe it was Walton or McLean—or—

RYAN

And what did he say?

BOYLE

He said, "Isn't it untrue that your Prime Minister's illness is not altogether physical?" or something like that. I honestly don't—

RYAN

And you said?

BOYLE

Yes.

Pause as F. X. tries to interpret this reply.

RYAN

Yes what?

BOYLE

Yes, it was untrue.

RYAN

So I'm bucking mental, is that it?

BOYLE

For God's sake, F.X.—!

RYAN *faces about, first simulating the tantrum and then genuinely experiencing it.*

RYAN

Good. Great. Wonderful. Thank you, Mister Minister. Thank you for your loyalty. The country on the threshold of a great new abyss—the people about to be plunged into a spiritual and economic depression—our youth crying out for dedicated and inspired leadership—and what does my Cabinet do? My Minister for Finance indulges in a whisper campaign about my health in foreign capitals! My Minister for External Affairs lies besotted in some squalid native ale house! My Minister for Defense is roistering at a funeral down the country! My Minister for Labor and my Minister for Education . . . (*He staggers, grabs the side of his desk, knocks over some papers, reels over toward the couch, and falls on it.*) Oh, my God . . . Drops—drops—give me the drops! On the desk . . . !

BOYLE *is alarmed and terrified.*

BOYLE

What—what—what's wrong? Steady, F.X., steady . . . (*Screams*) Sally!

RYAN

The drops on my desk—give them to me!

BOYLE

Sally! Quick! (*Frantic search.*) There's no drops here, F.X.—

SALLY *enters. She is calm; she has witnessed this scene many times before.*

Drops—he's looking for drops—there's none here—what do we do?

RYAN

Drops!

SALLY

A small bottle with a black top.

RYAN

Come on! Come on! Hurry up!

SALLY

It's not here, Mr. Ryan. You must have left it upstairs.

RYAN *opens his mouth and bellows at the top of his voice.*

RYAN

Maaaaa-meeeee!

BOYLE

Should—should—shouldn't we call a doctor?

SALLY

It only lasts a few minutes.

MRS. RYAN *enters carrying a tray with coffee.* NASH *is behind her. She is very old, very tiny, and lean as a whippet. To describe her as pixilated would be charitable: she was always a virago and now she is doting as well.*

Her son and herself have a peculiar relationship. When other people are present, he addresses her as crudely and insultingly as his vocabulary allows. She ignores this and treats him like a child. When they are alone together, his dependence on her is obvious and total.

MRS. RYAN

Shush-shush-shush-shush, mammy's coming, mammy's coming. (*She leaves the tray on the desk and goes to the couch.*)

RYAN

The drops, you bitch, the drops!

MRS. RYAN

Oh my poor, poor darling boy. Here we are. Everything's all right. Mammy has the drops for her darling Frankie.

RYAN

You bloody old cow—you hid them!

MRS. RYAN

Shush-shush, lie steady, atta good boy. Quiet—quiet.

RYAN

Bloody cow!

MRS. RYAN

Hold still—that's the way—not a move—mammy's going to drive that bad old dizziness away.

RYAN

Cow!

MRS. RYAN

Just one more tiny little drop—steady—now!

BOYLE *has been gazing in amazement at this domestic episode.*

NASH

You'll have a cup of coffee, Mr. Boyle?

BOYLE

What's that?

NASH

Coffee.

BOYLE

Oh yes. Yes, please. Delighted. If I may.

NASH

Do you feel like some coffee, Mr. Ryan?

MRS. RYAN

It was for him I made it.

RYAN

In a minute . . . Leave it there . . .

MRS. RYAN

(*Whispers*) They're still here. Get rid of them.

RYAN

Go to hell.

MRS. RYAN

Tinkers, dirtying up the whole house!

RYAN

Shut up.

MRS. RYAN

Leave them to me, then. I'll soon shift the tramps.

She wheels round and stares defiantly at BOYLE. *He smiles bleakly at her and then decides he had better speak.*

BOYLE

I think—I think we've met on a few occasions, Mrs. Ryan. Neil Boyle. (*Holds out his hand.*) Finance.

MRS. RYAN

I wouldn't give you a penny! An able-bodied man like you should be out digging up the roads instead of sponging on my boy's generosity!

NASH

Anybody want sugar?

BOYLE

Please, Roger.

MRS. RYAN

(*To* NASH) I have my eye on you, too!

NASH

(*To* SALLY) Sugar for Mr. Boyle.

MRS. RYAN

(*To* NASH) Yes, you, neat fellow! I'm watching you!

BOYLE

(*To* SALLY) Thank you, Sally.

MRS. RYAN

(*To* SALLY) And short skirts, too! I know you, child! I have your measure!

RYAN *now sits upright on the couch, shaking his head gently from side to side.*
The phone rings. NASH *answers it.*

NASH

Hallo.

RYAN

(*Gets unsteadily to his feet and comes down.*) Hits you like a bloody sledge hammer.

SALLY

Your coffee, Mr. Ryan.

RYAN

Thanks, Sally, thanks.

BOYLE

(*Cheerily*) You look normal enough, F.X.

RYAN

(*Withers him, then turns toward his mother*) And would you, for the love of God, leave those drops on my desk.

MRS. RYAN

Whatever you say, love. (*She goes to the desk and puts the drops into her pocket.*)

NASH

The Police Commissioner. The dockers have occupied the Law Courts.

BOYLE

Good Lord!

RYAN

And what does he want me to do—auction it for them?

NASH

He says he can't get in touch with the Minister of Justice.

RYAN

Has he gone into hiding, too? Give me that (*phone*).

F. X. Ryan here. Listen, Vincent, listen carefully. Get them out. Get them out at once.

MRS. RYAN

My boy can command.

RYAN

(*Furious*) I don't give a damn how you do it—that's your job. Do you know how to do mine? (*Brief pause.*) Right, then. Clear the building. (*He hangs up and wheels round.*) And if I'm not interrupting the party, maybe we could all get back to work now.

NASH

Incidentally, Mr. Ryan—

RYAN

What did you forget?

NASH

Just that the Archbishop rang before you came down.

MRS. RYAN

(*Coyly*) I told you—a papal knighthood! Sir Francis Xaviour! (*She skips off.*)

RYAN

Jeesus, you old—!

NASH

He's going to say Mass for you at 7:30 tomorrow morning.

RYAN

Why?

NASH

Why?

RYAN

Why for me and not for you or him (BOYLE) or her?

NASH

Because you—he just said—on account of your being—

RYAN

Unbalanced?

NASH

He didn't say that, Mr. Ryan.

BOYLE

If you'll excuse me, F.X. I'd like to go home and have a bath and something to eat. (*To* NASH) There's a Cabinet meeting this evening, isn't there?

NASH

Eight o'clock.

RYAN

If we can find the Ministers and if the Ministers can find the time.

BOYLE

There's no necessity for . . . We're all slightly on edge . . . (*As he gathers his things*) If you need me, I'll be at home all afternoon. (*In his confusion* BOYLE *gets the wrong coat.*)

NASH

I think that's the Taoiseach's coat, Mr. Boyle. (*He gives* BOYLE *the right coat.*)

BOYLE

See you tonight then . . . Thank you for the cup of coffee . . . Goodbye. (*He leaves rapidly.*)

SALLY *busies herself gathering up the cups.* NASH *pretends to examine papers.* RYAN *walks toward his desk, glances down into the wastepaper basket, and idly lifts out the top letter. He sits down and reads it.*

RYAN

". . . But Moloney, the Minister for External Affairs, and you, Ryan, is the biggest gangsters of all . . ." (*He drops the letter into the basket and gazes into the middle distance—the wounded, misinterpreted public figure.*) And the point is, Roger, that many of them honestly believe that. How long have I been in public service now—twenty-four, twenty-five years? You go into it as a young man, full of verve and vitality and vision. And why do you go into it? You go into it because you love your country

with a great, pulsating love; and you love the people of
your country with a great embracing charity. And you go
into it because—it sounds proud, may God forgive me,
but it isn't, it's the truth, and let the truth be spoken. You
go into it because you have a—a—a—concept of the kind
of society—a concept of the quality of life—your people
deserve—

NASH *answers the buzzer.*

NASH

Hello?

RYAN

(*Uninterrupted*) And you spend yourself—happily, eagerly, willingly—you spend yourself in trying to give realization to that concept, to that ideal. I don't have to be
told that I haven't succeeded in full. But all I can say is
that—

NASH

Mr. Moloney's here.

RYAN

(*Public man forgotten*) I'm going to kick his guts in. I'm
going to tear that hoor asunder.

NASH

Will I ask him to come in?

RYAN

(*Controlled*) Yes, Roger, ask him to come in.

NASH

(*On phone*) Show the Minister in, Sally.

RYAN

When did we last see him?

NASH

Six days ago.

RYAN

Or hear from him?

NASH

Not since then.

RYAN

Thank you, Roger.

RYAN *takes two pills and washes them down with water. Then he leans back in his seat, closes his eyes, wills himself into control.*

SALLY

(*At door*) The Minister for External Affairs.

MICHAEL MOLONEY *swings on, carrying a hold-all, two briefcases, and a document case. He is about the same age as* RYAN *but looks younger. He is dressed as* BOYLE *was dressed, but the formal clothes give* MOLONEY *no presence. His tie is askew, his collar open, his coat creased. He is small, dark, jaunty, irrepressible, loquacious, clever. He can sense an atmosphere and size up a situation in a second and his instinct for self-preservation is un-*

failing. One would never accuse him of being a Cabinet Minister: a publican, maybe, or a chirpy undertaker. His only political canon is: "When in danger, keep talking."

MOLONEY

God bless you, Sally. Well, would you look at who's sitting up there, the picture of health—and me expecting to be welcomed by a patient in his sickbed! F.X., how are you? Great to see you. Never saw you looking better. Hello, Roger. Case I forget, F.X., I bear fondest greetings from Bill and Lucy Schlesser of New York, from the Partridges of Amsterdam, and from Marie Lesseps in Brussels: their warmest love to you and to your mother. And the other item on the top of my head: the day before yesterday—or was it yesterday?—d'you know that for the past week I've spent on an average ten hours a day in planes—I don't know whether I'm coming or going— where was I? Yes, the other item: I have it on the best authority, F.X., that last year you were runner-up for the Nobel Peace Prize! What do you know about that? And if it comes to that—why not, I say? Right, Roger? (*He begins searching in his baggage.*)

RYAN

(*Quietly*) I gather, Michael, that since I saw you last, you've been in America and Belgium and Holland?

MOLONEY

Twice in New York. The second time I went straight from Rome. (*Searching*) I brought something back—

RYAN

And it never once occurred to you to report back? It never once struck you that you should let your department know where you were—(*loudly*) not to talk of giving your leader even an inkling of what the hell you've been up to for the past six days, gallivanting about the world while the country you represent is crumbling into goddamn pieces? You may go to the office, Roger.

NASH

Yes, sir.

NASH *leaves.* RYAN *is genuinely angry but is consciously playing the chief who can barely control his fury.*

RYAN

We've had our differences in the past, Moloney, and we've come through a lot together since the days when I was learning the auctioneering racket and you were a turf accountant's clerk—

MOLONEY

Bookie's runner.

RYAN

—but I'm damned if I'm going to take any more cavalier treatment from you or from anybody bloody else. Never in all my years in public life have I encountered such shabbiness and—and—and—and—downright disloyalty from my colleagues. But by you, Moloney, I've been virtually insulted. And I demand an apology. And I demand an explanation. And if you're not prepared to give me both, I demand your resignation—now.

MOLONEY

(*Abjectly*) My God, F.X., I'm sorry. Of course, of *course* I should have phoned you—my God, it's the very least I could have done. And I did intend to—several times— but that's no excuse, no excuse at all. The point is I didn't —only because I wanted to tell you the good news in person. And now you're hurt. And you're right to be hurt. And I'm totally in the wrong. And I apologize humbly to you, F.X., humbly.

RYAN *scarcely knows how to accept this. He holds on to gruffness.*

RYAN

Very well, Mick, I accept that apology.

MOLONEY

As for the explanation . . . In the past six days I have negotiated—subject to your approval, of course; everything is dependent on your ratification—but I have negotiated an agreement for the biggest and most revolutionary and most rewarding commercial transaction that this country has ever undertaken. (*Producing bottle*) Ah, here we are, Scotch. Made specially for Francis Ferdinand in 1910. Have you a couple of glasses? (RYAN *pushes the glasses over.*) Thanks. Yes, I nipped into the office on the way here and I gather things are pretty bad. But, as they say, F.X., every cloud . . . And the lining of this one's pure gold. (*Raises his glass.*) To the Mundy Scheme. (*He drinks.* RYAN *stares at him and does not touch his glass.*)

RYAN

The explanation.

MOLONEY

The explanation . . . Frank, what would you say to a flood of capital investment into the country, an immediate drop in emigration, full employment in depressed areas, new airstrips capable of carrying the biggest jets, a 300 percent leap in tourism—

RYAN

Moloney, I—

MOLONEY

—to a transformation of the whole barren west into the most wealthy and most productive part of the country, to—

RYAN

(*Almost shouting*) I'd say no; that's what I'd say: no, no, no, no, no! (*Softly*) Moloney, listen to me, Moloney. I'm a sick man; I've been under enormous strain for the past four months. Maybe I'm no longer competent to lead the

Irish people, and if they so decide that they'd prefer a different captain at the helm I'll willingly bow to their decision and be content to dedicate whatever talent is left in me to giving service below deck. (*Loud again*) But as long as I'm boss of this goddamn sinking curragh, there'll be no American nuclear subs, no American communication centers, and no American military or naval supply bases on our shores. Maybe we're insignificant; but at least we're clean of this dirty nuclear game. And that's the way we're going to stay! (*Drinks rapidly.*)

MOLONEY *gazes alertly: what is* RYAN *talking about.*

MOLONEY

F.X., you have just delivered a major speech on our domestic and foreign policies.

RYAN

Boyle couldn't see it either. But give the American forces one foothold here and you couldn't begin to give away our exports in Europe. (*To stop* MOLONEY *filling his glass again*) No more for me.

MOLONEY

An extra tot of rum never killed the skipper. And the skipper's going to be skipper for one hell of a long time to come. (*Fills both glasses and toasts.*) God bless, Frank.

RYAN

Luck.

MOLONEY
Beautiful stuff.

Silence.

RYAN
So that's what you've been up to?

MOLONEY
What?

RYAN
Making a deal with the Pentagon?

MOLONEY
I've been negotiating a *real* deal. (*He sits forward.*) Remember a man called Homer Mundy?

RYAN
No.

MOLONEY
Texan—Irish-American—Homer Mundy, Jr.

RYAN
Never heard of him.

MOLONEY
'Course you did. I introduced him to you three years ago in Rome.

RYAN

A blank.

MOLONEY

Tall, solemn, completely bald, middle-aged. Head of Mundy Real Estate Incorporated. Multimillionaire.

RYAN

No memory.

MOLONEY

You must have—we used to joke about him—the fellow who had all his ancestors disinterred and reburied in County Sligo where the family came from originally away back in the famine.

RYAN

Not the character with the tiny wife?—the big lunatic with the rimless glasses that—?

MOLONEY

The very man. And that character is now one of the top advisers in Washington. And make no mistake about it, F.X., he's no lunatic. In fact, he's about as shrewd a businessman as I've ever come across: the highest ground landlord in Manhattan and the biggest real-estate agent in the whole East Coast.

RYAN

I should have emigrated when I was young.

MOLONEY

I've been with him all day, every day, for the past week. And we've hammered out a plan—and I promise you, F.X., this is no harebrained scheme—I've got concrete commitments here (*briefcase*) from New York, London, Brussels, Paris, and Amsterdam—an industrial development scheme that's all ready to go if we can sell it to the Cabinet—a plan that will transform this country overnight—nothing whatever to do with subs or rockets or bases or anything like that—a straight commercial proposition. (*He sits back. Pause.*)

RYAN

I'm listening.

MOLONEY

You haven't touched your drink.

RYAN *drinks.* MOLONEY *fills the glasses again.*

RYAN

Well?

MOLONEY *opens his briefcase, takes out some papers, closes the case. He leans forward and lifts a black marker off the desk.*

MOLONEY

May I?

RYAN *gestures consent.* MOLONEY *rises and crosses to the map on the wall.*

MOLONEY

Phase One. (*He turns to the map and inks out with black ink the western half of County Mayo. Then he turns to* RYAN.)

Phase Two. (*This time he blacks out the rest of Mayo, County Sligo, and Connemara. Again he turns to* RYAN.)

Phase Three. (*This time he blacks out all of Galway, all Roscommon, and all of Leitrim. Now he comes back to the desk, leaves the marker down, and takes a drink.*)

RYAN

The great scheme, Mick—when you're ready.

MOLONEY

The Homer Mundy International Incorporated Proposal —hereafter referred to as the Mundy Scheme—is divided into three phases. Phase One deals specifically with the western half of County Mayo, excluding all offshore islands but including Achill. Phase Two deals with the remainder of Mayo, Connemara and Sligo. Phase Three deals with the remainder of Galway, all Roscommon, and all Leitrim. These three phases will take care of a total area not exceeding six thousand square miles and not less than five thousand square miles. Tentative provision is also made for a Phase Four, making Donegal and Clare optional extras.

RYAN

Mick—

MOLONEY

But the terms and specifications will apply fully to each phase of the operation and the annuity proposed and mutually agreed to will be subject to review every five years —provided both licensee and licensor make written request—

RYAN

Mick—Mick—

MOLONEY

—for such review. Yes, F.X.?

RYAN

The great scheme—in simple language.

MOLONEY

In simple language—

RYAN

And briefly.

MOLONEY

Briefly and simply, they will lease all the land in the west that is uneconomic to farm, and they're offering us a hundred cool dollars per acre per annum—mountains, bogs, hills—a flat rate for everything.

RYAN

For industrial development?

MOLONEY

(*Tossing paper on desk*) A contract for Phase One with a non-returnable deposit of half a million dollars. And there's the check.

RYAN

Bogs? Hills?

MOLONEY

An initial lease of fifty years, subject to review every five years.

RYAN

And what in the name of God do they propose to manufacture?

MOLONEY

The terms specifically exclude all lands within a three-mile radius of any town or village with a population of sixty persons or more, and all lands within a quarter of a mile radius of individual houses, homes, factories, churches, or business premises.

RYAN

Mick—

MOLONEY

The lands will be held by Homer Mundy Incorporated Ireland, a subsidiary company which will hold its meetings here, be subject to Irish taxation, and have on its board five Irish nationals and three Americans.

RYAN

Mick, I—

MOLONEY

All territories will be preserved in their natural state except when landscaping would be desirable, and the building of all roads, airstrips, and communication links—and the upkeep of these—will be financed fully by the company. Of course, all existing right-of-ways will be respected and—

RYAN

(*Shouts*) Moloney!

MOLONEY

F.X.

RYAN

May I speak?

MOLONEY

By all means.

RYAN

A simple question from a simple man: what in the name of the good God does the Homer Mundy Irish Consolidated International Incorporated Limited want with bloody bogs?

MOLONEY

The very thing I was coming to, F.X. As I told you, our friend is the biggest real-estate man in the East Coast of America. Now he points out that the most valuable ground in the world is ground in and around the centers of the big cities—London, Paris, New York. Correct?

RYAN

Go on.

MOLONEY

And as those cities spread, ground becomes more scarce and therefore more expensive. For example, in the heart of New York City there are sites that are worth £120 per square foot. And yet in all these large cities some of the most valuable land is at present occupied by cemeteries; and as these cities expand, more and more cemeteries are required.

RYAN

So?

MOLONEY

So, Mundy argues, let's look to the future. Let's create a new trend.

RYAN

I don't know what the hell you're driving at, but I've had enough—

MOLONEY

France is the recognized home of good food; America is the acknowledged center of art; Switzerland is the center of Europe's banking. Let's make the west of Ireland the acknowledged . . . eternal resting place.

RYAN

You mean . . . ?

MOLONEY

We can supply the very commodity these big cities need —ground, thousands of acres of it—useless ground—crying out for development.

RYAN *is absolutely stunned. He rises very slowly, never taking his eyes from* MOLONEY, *and moves down-stage. Then he turns and points to the map. When he speaks, his voice is almost a whisper.*

RYAN

A graveyard?

MOLONEY

For the Western capitals. We have everything: ideal situation, suitable climate, religious atmosphere—the lot. F.X. Believe me, F.X., this is the answer to all our problems.

RYAN *moves slowly up-stage, almost as if he were in concussion. Then he falters, takes another step, staggers. Then he stands still.*

Silence. Suddenly he lurches toward the couch and, as he goes, shouts at the top of his voice.

RYAN

Drops! Drops! Give me the drops . . . !

CURTAIN

ACT TWO

The small hours of the following morning. RYAN, MOLONEY, BOYLE, *and the two other Ministers,* DAN MAHON *and* CHARLES HOGAN, *have been discussing the Mundy Scheme for eight exhausting hours and are spent and irritable. They have argued for so long and so circuitously that they have arrived at the point when all that has been said is a blur.*

DAN MAHON, *Minister for Development, is from the west, heavily built, physically very strong, in his early sixties. His mind is blunt, tenacious, and untutored. He works tirelessly for his constituents and has earned his place in the Cabinet because of his enormous influence and popularity "down the country." He believes in speaking his mind, putting his cards on the table, and getting the record straight—exercises that to him are synonymous with the practice of virtue. He is a thick.*

CHARLES HOGAN, *Minister for Commerce, is in his seventies and almost on the brink of senility. He is no longer capable of following a discussion of any intricacy but has occasional reflexive illuminations when certain words like "God" or "womenfolk" or "vote" crop up. He was once a "young bull" like Mahon and admires the species inordinately.*

When the curtain rises, HOGAN *is fast asleep on the couch.* MAHON *is pacing up and down, his brain alert and vibrant with suspicion because he is convinced that he is being hoodwinked in some way—and he is terrified of appearing foolish in public.*

BOYLE *has shrunken more than ever. He is cold and tired and sits alone, hugging his elbows and gazing fixedly at the floor.*

RYAN, *in his shirt sleeves, sits on the corner of his desk, passing a paperweight from one hand to the other.*

MOLONEY, *down-stage right, is working at calculations that require all his concentration (although a portion of his mind knows precisely what every man in the room is doing). He is completely calm and self-contained. His spectacles give him a professional look. Silence, except for the nervous pacing of* MAHON.

RYAN

My watch has stopped. Anybody got the time?

MAHON *pauses and looks around suspiciously.*

BOYLE

The time? Oh, yes, the time . . . It's—it's—4:30. Soon be daybreak.

RYAN

Thank you.

He winds his watch. MAHON *begins pacing.*

BOYLE

I hope we're not disturbing your mother.

MAHON *stops.*

RYAN

No, no, she's asleep hours ago.

MAHON *paces.*

BOYLE

(*With shrill irritation*) Would the Minister of Development please—

MAHON *stops and stares defiantly at him.*

(*More quietly*)—please have a seat.

MAHON *stares at him for a second and then resumes pacing. Knock.* NASH *enters from office.*

NASH

More coffee, gentlemen?

RYAN

Please, Roger . . . Roger, a minute. (*Whispers to him*) Where is she?

NASH

In the kitchen, sir.

MOLONEY

(*Looks up from his papers.*) A small point I should have mentioned, gentlemen: we forfeit mineral rights but retain grazing. (*He smiles benignly, puts on his glasses, and goes back to work.*)

RYAN

(*Whispers*) What's she doing?

NASH

Making marmalade.

RYAN

Marmalade?

NASH

Orange. She says she'll bring some in for you to taste.

RYAN

God.

NASH

Even though it won't be set, she says.

MAHON

(*Belligerently*) If you ask me, what's brought us to our knees is all the secret, furtive, surreptitious dealing that's going on behind backs! A bit of honesty and plain talking for a change and we mightn't be in the mess we're in.

RYAN

My private secretary was merely intimating to me that my mother is preserving marmalade.

MAHON *looks at his watch—marmalade at this hour?—and raises his eyebrows in mockery.*

And I would suggest, Dan, that as Minister for Development, you bear proportionate responsibility for the mess, as you call it. The coffee, Roger.

NASH

(*Leaving*) Yes, sir.

MAHON

As my mother—God be good to her—used to say, "If he whispers, he's a twister."

BOYLE

May I propose, F.X.—we've argued this Mundy Scheme all night and have arrived at no conclusion—so may I propose that we adjourn for a day or two until we all have slept on it, and then we—

MAHON

You want to know what I think of his (MOLONEY) plan?

RYAN

You've already given us an inkling.

BOYLE

—and then we could convene a full meeting of the Cabinet and—

MAHON

I think it's the maddest, most ridiculous, most outrageous scheme I've ever heard. And when word gets out that we actually sat up half the bloody night discussing it, we'll be the laughing stock of the world—that's what we'll be.

BOYLE

—and—and get a consensus of—

RYAN

Thank you, Mr. Mahon.

BOYLE

—opinion—

MAHON

It's all very well for you to sit tight and take no sides, F.X., but as Minister for Development it would be my pigeon right along the line. Seventeen years ago you made me responsible for that bankrupt baby-powder factory in Castlebar and they called me Delivery Dan ever since. But I'm damned if I'll go down in history as Mortuary Mahon.

RYAN

So, the Minister for Development is unsympathetic to the Mundy Scheme.

MAHON

Wrong. Anti.

RYAN

The Minister for Finance?

BOYLE

Am I going to be permitted to speak? As I attempted to say earlier, I'm against making a firm decision tonight— this morning—at this moment—

RYAN

Wait a week and we're out of office.

BOYLE

And I have already put to the Cabinet the offer from the Pentagon, which, I suggest, is much less ambiguous and at least as beneficial to the country as a—

MAHON

We had trouble enough getting rid of the English. And you can take it from me here and now we're going to have no dirty Yankee sailors with nuclear warheads se-ducing decent Galway girls and decent Cork girls.

BOYLE

Mr. Chairman—!

MAHON

If God hasn't said it, you'll be wanting ports for the Rus-sians next, and then be Jaysus we'll have to call out the army to protect our grandmothers! (*Shaking* HOGAN) Wake up, Charlie! They're at the women!

HOGAN

(*Waking up*) Women!

BOYLE

I object . . . !

HOGAN

Dan Mahon's right. Whatever Dan says, I say!

BOYLE

For heaven's sake, F.X.

MAHON

We won't stand for it!

BOYLE

If you can't control the meeting, then close it. It's utterly impossible to think constructively in this atmosphere.

MAHON

You'll close nothing.

HOGAN

Hear hear. And as Minister for Commerce I demand—

Everyone is shouting at once. Uproar. RYAN *quiets them.*

RYAN

Mr. Hogan, please. Charlie, please . . . please . . . Dan . . . Neil . . . Gentlemen, please, sit down, sit down . . .

We're overwrought! We're all tired. And if the measure of a strong government is its behavior under duress—extreme duress—then this is our testing time. Let's measure up to it, gentlemen.

A knock. NASH *enters with tray of coffee, etc.*

NASH
Early breakfast, gentlemen!

RYAN
Good man, Roger! This is what we need, boys!

NASH *starts to distribute coffee.* RYAN *takes a cup for* MOLONEY *and calls him over.*

RYAN
I told you.

MOLONEY
Easy.

RYAN
I warned you they'd never bite.

MOLONEY
Don't rush them.

RYAN
Rush them!

MOLONEY

Mahon's confused. Look at him.

RYAN

Plowman.

MOLONEY

A little flattery and he's with us. I'll handle this.

RYAN

You'll not move Boyle.

MOLONEY

No difficulty.

RYAN

He won't make up his mind.

MOLONEY

He'll follow the herd.

RYAN

Maybe we should wait till morning.

MOLONEY

And give them time to think?

RYAN

I can't hold them all night.

MOLONEY

Shhh.

RYAN

It's up to you, Moloney.

MOLONEY

Leave it to me then; they're about to break.

RYAN

Well now . . . Neil, you had the floor—you were about to say?

BOYLE

Do I take it that the American proposal is rejected?

HOGAN

Which one?

MAHON

They both stink.

BOYLE

The Pentagon Proposal.

MAHON

It is.

HOGAN

Completely!

RYAN

Let's stick to Mr. Moloney's scheme for the time being.

BOYLE

In that case I withdraw from any further discussion to-night—this morning.

MAHON

Good.

BOYLE

But I wish to make one final point. You may have moral or practical reservations about granting facilities to the American armed forces—

HOGAN

We have both.

BOYLE

—but I ask you to consider, and consider seriously, what this bizarre Mundy Scheme may do to the national psyche. We are addicted to death as it is. A lot of our literature, our music, our legends, the whole emphasis of our religion—all revolve around death and the dead. And I warn you, if you adopt this plan, you will push us further into this morass. And I promise you, F.X., I solemnly promise you, you will end up with a nation of chronic necrophiliacs.

MAHON

God bless us and save us!

RYAN

A nice point, Neil.

HOGAN

Chronic what-what-what?

RYAN

Very well put.

HOGAN

A nation of what?

RYAN

The Minister is concerned about the future of our literature and music and religion . . . And I'm sure you'll all
agree that a nation without these things is . . . is . . . is
in a very unhealthy state indeed. I share your anxiety,
Neil.

HOGAN

I don't know what you're talking about; and I still don't
know where you stand on the Mundy Scheme, F.X.

RYAN

Me?

MAHON

On the fence.

RYAN

That's unfair.

HOGAN

Are you for it or against it?

MAHON

He always does the same thing—knocks us down to the highest bidder.

RYAN

Another crack like that from you, Mahon!

HOGAN

For or against?

MAHON

You're wasting your time, Charlie.

BOYLE

I propose we adjourn.

RYAN

(*Shouts*) We adjourn when I say we adjourn, and not one second sooner! I'm still head of this government. I'm still Taoiseach of this country. And I've endured enough insolence and insubordination for one night! So sit down and shut up!

Everyone sits. Total silence.

(*Quietly, with dignity*) I now call on Mr. Michael Moloney, Minister for External Affairs, to give us a brief summary of his case. We will then take a vote—

MAHON

With half the Cabinet missing?

RYAN

—and when I have the views of my colleagues, I will give them careful consideration and arrive at my own decision. Mr. Moloney . . .

MAHON, *to show his complete indifference, lifts a newspaper.*

MAHON

(*Bitterly*) Nothing like the democratic process. (*To* HOGAN) Have you a bed with your Auntie Nellie?

HOGAN

I have, Dan.

HOGAN

Not that you'll need it.

MOLONEY *rises, spectacles in one hand, documents in the other. He moves into a dominant position. He is about to give a performance.*

MOLONEY

Thank you, F.X.

Taoiseach, fellow Ministers, I find myself in a strange position. I find myself acting as defense counsel on behalf of a scheme that I thought—I was sure—would have been grasped at with both hands, considering the critical state our country is in.

But after listening to the various views expressed here to-night, I realize now, of course, that when I explained the Mundy Scheme to you, I concentrated far too much on niggling details and not nearly enough on the general shape. From your pertinent comments, Dan, it's obvious that *you've* got a comprehensive grasp of the whole picture; and God knows how you have, because I was far too technical.

Gentlemen, as you well know, I come from humble origins. I was the youngest of fourteen children, and my good father, may he rest in peace, had a six-acre farm—

HOGAN

And five greyhounds.

MOLONEY

—so that when I talk about hunger, Taoiseach, I'm not talking about something I've read: and when I speak of cold and poverty and humiliation, I'm not speaking of some far-off country on the other side of the globe. And conditions such as these—although not perhaps to the same degree—still exist in our fair land to this day. So I ask myself a single question. I say to myself: What would my good father have said if someone had come to him with a simple proposal such as this? If someone had said to him, Mr. Moloney, you have a farm of worthless land, and despite your greatest efforts you cannot wring even a meager living from it: four of your sons and three of your daughters have had to emigrate; you live in penury, in isolation, in loneliness. Mr. Moloney, I am prepared to rent your land—or as many acres as you are prepared to give me. I will fence these worthless fields and drain them. I will construct broad, sweeping roads alongside those worthless fields. I will bring visitors, tourists by the hundred, along those broad, sweeping roads, and your little remote holding will no longer be isolated, alone, lonely on the rim of Western Europe but will be right in the mainstream of world commerce, world thought, world action. Mr. Moloney, is this what you want? A place in the open society, dignity and prosperity for yourself, your neighbors, your country? Is this what you choose, Mr. Moloney? Gentlemen, not for one second do I doubt what my father's reply would be. And if there is a man in this room who has a doubt for any reason whatsoever —either because he is nervous of change or because he is thinking selfishly of his own political skin—I say to that man here and now: Go to Connemara, go to West Donegal, go to Achill, Belmullet, Kilrush, and ask the decent people there—what do you want? decay or development, emigration or affluence, penury or prosperity, misery or Mundy? And I promise you that doubt will soon be dispelled.

Neil Boyle, you know what I'm talking about. So do you, Charlie Hogan. So do you, Taoiseach. But the man who knows best, who knows even better than I do, is Dan Mahon, because the west of Ireland made him what he is,

and in return he wants nothing but the best for the west
of Ireland.

Gentlemen, our country is in agony. And it seems to me
that we have two alternatives. We can say: we abdicate,
we resign, we have run out of ideas and dedication, we
have nothing more to give. Or, gentlemen, we can say:
Ireland, I stand by you, I will see you through your labor,
I will nurse you back to health and vigor and glory. The
choice is ours, gentlemen. If our economy were buoyant,
the Mundy Scheme would still be welcome. As it is, I
think it is nothing short of miraculous. Thank you.

RYAN

Thank *you,* Mick. A very calm and very informative ex-
position. Well, gentlemen, there it is. If there's still anything troubling you, now's your time to speak. But I'll
tell you something: it would be bloody rich if I could go
to the President with this scheme and with your full approval of it before the deputation from the opposition gets
to him and demands our resignation—eh?

NASH

(*At door*) Excuse me—

RYAN

Yes?

NASH

The Commissioner phoned. He has fortified the Law
Courts and assures you it won't be taken again.

RYAN

Good.

NASH

Casualties on both sides, he says, but you'll have no more trouble with the dockers for many a day.

RYAN

Thanks, Roger.

NASH *leaves.*

(*To* OTHERS) The tide's on the turn, boys! Right—are you all behind Mick?

MAHON

It's all very well for him (MOLONEY): his seat isn't affected. But I'll represent a bloody graveyard.

MOLONEY

(*Consulting papers*) In rents alone, Dan, your constituency will be the second wealthiest in the country—and you'll have ancillary benefits on top of that.

HOGAN

How do these—these remains come?

MOLONEY

By air to Dublin—until they build the airstrip in Achill.

MAHON
How often?

MOLONEY
One plane per week from New York and one plane per week from Paris—that's to start with.

HOGAN
When they arrive, will they be—you know—all set for—

MOLONEY
In caskets manufactured here and made under license issued exclusively by you as Minister for Commerce.

MAHON
And we just bury them?

MOLONEY
One of our responsibilities is to supply crematoria—

HOGAN
What?

MOLONEY
—and I've arranged that they'll be fueled by turf.

BOYLE
Two planeloads a week?

MOLONEY
Guaranteed. And that's only a beginning. Until we really sell the idea that an all-inclusive package-deal burial in

Ireland is cheaper than buying a plot in New York and being buried there.

BOYLE

Is the—are the—the—?

MOLONEY

Let's call it freight.

BOYLE

Is it subject to import duty?

MOLONEY

I'll have to get a ruling on that, Neil. Had the freight come unpacked, it would certainly be subject to import duty. But since it arrives packaged and sealed in containers previously manufactured in this country, under Section 73a of the 1933 Act, it may be deemed a reimported export—and consequently not subject to duty.

BOYLE

A big loss.

MOLONEY

We'll make up for it with the containers, which are shipped out on the empty planes.

MAHON

Where do they want to start?

MOLONEY

Achill.

BOYLE

Payments in dollars or sterling?

MOLONEY

Dollars. Even the European shipments will be paid for from the U.S.

HOGAN

Why didn't you get England roped in too?

MOLONEY

I did.

HOGAN

You said New York and Paris.

MOLONEY

The Paris plane stops in London on the way here.

HOGAN

Be God!

MAHON

You and I can comprehend it all, Mick (*a lie*): but country people would be frightened off with leases and legal papers and—

MOLONEY

But we do all that for them. We vest their land and the
company deals directly with us.

BOYLE

We'll need time.

MOLONEY

What for?

BOYLE

Push new legislation through.

MOLONEY

What legislation?

BOYLE

To vest whole counties—ultimately a whole province.

MOLONEY

Why present it that way? All we're doing is vesting a
farm here and a farm here and a farm there.

BOYLE

But—

MOLONEY

And existing legislation covers that, doesn't it?

MAHON

And who pays the people?

MOLONEY

We do.

HOGAN

A hundred dollars an acre.

MOLONEY

Less stamp duty and turnover tax and 5 percent commission.

MAHON

What commission?

MOLONEY

Ours—agent's fees. It's going to be an enormous undertaking for your department, Dan. Can you handle it?

MAHON

Never fell down on a job yet.

MOLONEY

(*To* RYAN) His staff will have to be doubled.

MAHON

Doubled?

MOLONEY

At least.

RYAN

No problem.

BOYLE

Any reaction from Russia?

MOLONEY

Interest, but no commitment.

BOYLE

No political objections?

MOLONEY

Not that I know of.

RYAN

(*Prompting* MOLONEY) Sanctuary.

MOLONEY

Oh, yes, they did remark that in the event of war this
scheme endows us with sanctuary status and provides us
with complete immunity.

HOGAN

Like a big church.

MAHON

Holy ground.

MOLONEY

Exactly.

BOYLE

What about industrial plants already functioning in these
areas?

MOLONEY

What about them?

BOYLE

They may not like . . . their new environment.

MOLONEY

Mr. Chairman—?

RYAN

Mick and I have discussed that point, Neil. If they want to move out, the government will facilitate them as best we can.

MOLONEY

And all new industries that are not associated with the scheme, we'll encourage them to set up in the eastern half of the country. Wouldn't you agree, Dan?

MAHON

Indeed—yes—of course—that would be my intention.

HOGAN

But if most of the west is covered with headstones, F.X., surely to God this will destroy our tourist industry there.

MOLONEY

On the contrary, I estimate that our tourist trade will be trebled at least. Not only will we still get the people who come here for a quiet, restful holiday—in fact, we now hope to get thousands more—but we will also get regular visits from the friends and relations of the people who are buried here. (*To* F.X.) Charlie'll need much bigger office space and probably another assistant secretary.

RYAN

No difficulty. And the demand for hotels, souvenir shops, flowers, wreaths, headstones, railings—it's going to be overwhelming.

MOLONEY

And this is the kind of light industry that the west will attract.

RYAN

There could well be a labor shortage.

MOLONEY

No, no, the immediate halt in emigration will supply that.

RYAN

And the return of emigrants already gone.

MOLONEY

True.

BOYLE

You've certainly done your homework, Michael.

MOLONEY

Thank you, Neil. There's a lot at stake.

MAHON

By God, it all fits together like a jigsaw.

MOLONEY

And, gentlemen, two planes a week is only the hors d'oeuvre. When we really get going, two planes per day will be landing right in the west.

RYAN *knows that now is the time to clinch agreement.*

RYAN

In a nutshell, boys, the Mundy Scheme is a heart transplant at a critical time. It means a flood of capital investment, an immediate drop in emigration, full employment in depressed areas, new airstrips capable of carrying the biggest—

MRS. RYAN *marches in with a pot of marmalade in one hand and an outstretched spoon in the other. She is in her dressing gown and slippers.*

RYAN

Mother! For God's sake—

She ignores everyone else and heads straight for her son. The others get to their feet and mumble good night.

Not now, you stupid bitch! Get to hell up to bed!

MRS. RYAN

Taste it. I made it for you.

RYAN

You're for the Nazareth House in the morning!

MRS. RYAN

It's still a bit warm, but it's very nice.

RYAN *is furious—embarrassed. He hustles her to the door and keeps glancing over his shoulder in case he is overheard. He tastes the marmalade.*

RYAN

Lovely, now get out—get out!

MRS. RYAN

Are they troublesome?

RYAN

Please—

MRS. RYAN

Will I call the guards?

RYAN

I'm warning you, you weasel, I'll strangle you!

MRS. RYAN

I made sixteen pounds. I've still to put the labels and the date on them.

RYAN

For God's sake—

MRS. RYAN

Did you get rid of that woman?

RYAN

Everything's under control.

MRS. RYAN

The typist with the short skirt—she's got her eye on you.

RYAN

Out—out—out.

MRS. RYAN

Nothing she'd like better than to be married to a Papal Knight. Where's Roger Nash?

RYAN

This is a very important meeting—

MRS. RYAN

He made suggestions to me this morning.

RYAN

I'll kill you.

MRS. RYAN

Dirty suggestions.

RYAN

Out, bag—out—out—out.

MRS. RYAN

I'm going. (*Turning and looking at* BOYLE) I know his face.

BOYLE

(*Embarrassed*) Mrs. Ryan . . . how are you?

MRS. RYAN

No. Not as much as one penny. (*To* RYAN) Nighty-night, son.

RYAN

Good night, good night.

She marches off.

Sorry about that, boys . . . Where were we?

MOLONEY

May I say one last thing, F.X.?

RYAN

Please.

MOLONEY

No, two things. In my estimate we're sitting on an oil well. It may be big. It may be enormous. At this stage, none of us can tell. But at its minimum it's going to mean that we will be able to afford our program for health, housing, social welfare, and education. And when we do that we'll stay in power for—well, let's say for our time.

RYAN

And that's as long as we want. Any questions? Neil?

BOYLE *spreads his hands.*

RYAN

Dan?

MAHON

I think that under the circumstances, F.X., I'm reasonably satisfied.

RYAN

Charlie?

HOGAN

Shouldn't we get the views of the rest of the Cabinet?

RYAN *and* MOLONEY *exchange a quick glance.*

RYAN

If the plan were a deviation from agreed Cabinet policy, Charlie, then I'd be duty-bound to consult all my colleagues. But since the Mundy Scheme is really a practical résumé of our policy for the west—and since only three or four Ministries are directly involved—I think we should make this decision ourselves.

MOLONEY

Good point.

RYAN

(*Breezily*) And now that you are all for it, boys, now our real job begins—how to present it as attractively and persuasively as possible.

MAHON

How will the trade unions take it?

HOGAN

And the banks?

RYAN

And the Church?

MOLONEY

Not tonight, F.X., please. Couldn't we get a few hours' sleep before we go into that?

BOYLE

I second that, Michael.

MOLONEY

Let's meet again in the morning when we're fresher.

RYAN

Okay—whatever you say. What about ten o'clock?

MOLONEY

Eleven.

RYAN

Eleven it is. Here in the house. Thank you, boys. It's been a good night's work. (*To* BOYLE) You must be exhausted, Neil.

BOYLE

Permanent condition.

RYAN

Many's the time we've burned the midnight oil, gentlemen. But never before have we burned it so—so—so constructively.

HOGAN

See you in the morning, F.X.

RYAN

Thank you, Charlie. Thank you, Dan. Oh—gentlemen—gentlemen!

They all stop.

There's no need to impress on you—*total* silence. One syllable of what transpired here tonight gets out and every con man and speculator in the country is alerted.

MOLONEY

Not a word.

MAHON

F.X.

RYAN

Daniel, you look worried.

MAHON

You're sure there'll be no penny-pinching when it comes to staffing my department?

RYAN

For heaven's sake, Dan, you're our golden goose!

MAHON

That's good enough for me. I'll not let you down, F.X.

RYAN

Take care. Good men are scarce.

MOLONEY

I forgot to tell you, boys! Relatives who wish to accompany their freight on the plane get a rock-bottom rate.

HOGAN

That's a good idea.

MOLONEY

And the scheme is being advertised under the tag line: *Rest In Peace in Ireland*.

HOGAN

Or, what about the *West's A Wake*—d'you get it, eh?

RYAN

Thank you all again. Eleven sharp. God bless. Safe home. Sleep well.

They all bid their goodbyes—all except MOLONEY *who busies himself with his belongings.*

(*Using the intercom*) Roger.

ROGER *appears at the door.*

NASH

Yes?

RYAN

Sorry for holding you up, Roger.

NASH

That's all right, Mr. Ryan.

RYAN

Have a sleep in the morning. I won't need you until— say, 10:30.

NASH

I'll be here at nine as usual.

RYAN

You've been a tower of strength, Roger. God bless.

NASH

Good night, sir.

NASH *leaves.* MOLONEY *closes the door after him and turns to face* RYAN. *They gaze at one another with incredulous delight.*

MOLONEY

Didn't I tell you!

RYAN

Hook, line, and bloody sinker!

They meet and grip hands and embrace.

Be Jaysus, but you're a right hoor too!

MOLONEY

(*Innocent*) Me?

RYAN

You and your poor father!

MOLONEY

With his fourteen children!

RYAN

And his six-acre farm!

MOLONEY

The only green he ever knew was on a snooker table!

RYAN

I knew Mahon and Hogan would swallow that guff, but I didn't think Boyle would!

MOLONEY

He thinks he's an intellectual; facts impress him.

RYAN

You're a goddamn crafty bastard, Moloney!

MOLONEY

Crafty?

RYAN

And by God I admire you!

MOLONEY

We pulled it off, didn't we?

RYAN

You did! You were bloody great!

MOLONEY

"I'll not let you down, F.X."

RYAN

Bog-trotter.

MOLONEY

Well, Francis Xaviour, they're with us.

RYAN

They're with us, Michael.

MOLONEY

Whatever about the public.

RYAN

Whatever about the public.

MOLONEY

We'll swing them, too. All a matter of selling.

RYAN

You'll have a drink, Mick.

MOLONEY

Not for me.

RYAN

Just one. One to celebrate.

MOLONEY

I'm for bed. Now that it's all over, I'm about to drop.

RYAN

(*Politician's sincerity*) Thank you, Mick. You did a great job.

MOLONEY

The race isn't over yet.

RYAN

It's as good as. I'd put my shirt on it. Wouldn't you?

MOLONEY

Ex-bookies don't gamble. Good night, F.X.

RYAN

Good night, Mick. See you in the morning. And thanks again.

MOLONEY *leaves.* RYAN *stands thinking for a few seconds. Then he pours himself a drink, sits down at his desk, takes two pills, and washes them down with whisky. He is very content with things. He lifts the phone. Dials Operator.*

RYAN

Dublin 60093752. I want to make a personal call to Ballybeg 193. (*Pause.*) Personal to Mr. Declan Ryan, auctioneer. (*Pause.*) No, I don't wish to say who's calling. (*As he waits for the call to come through, he smiles into his glass.*) Declan? F.X. here. How's the big heart, Declan? And Delia and the kids? . . . Great, great.

MOLONEY *has returned and starts listening just inside the door.*

Sorry to waken you at this hour of the morning, Declan, but there's something I want you to do for me immediately. Get Delia's brother—no, not the married one; the single fellow, the teacher, Kieran that's him, the one that bought the dance hall for us—get him to drive down to Meenmore and take an option on as much land as he can get his hands on right up the length of Ballymore and away out to the sea . . . Yes, immediately . . . Anything, everything. I'm not fussy: hills, bogs, rough, anything . . . No, not you yourself—the firm's name mustn't be associated with it—is that perfectly clear? . . . Let Kieran use his discretion: some of it he'll pick up for a tenner an acre and some he'll have to go up to . . . Right. That's the very idea . . . No, don't ring me back. I'll call you sometime tomorrow afternoon and explain it all to you . . . Yes, as much as he can lay hands on. And remember, our name . . . Good boy, Declan, fine. Give my love to Delia. 'Bye. (*He hangs up.*)

MOLONEY

I thought you'd be quick off the mark, F.X.

RYAN *swings round.*

RYAN

Mick . . .

MOLONEY

That's a dangerous game, you know.

RYAN

Mick, aul son, is it you? D'you know what I was doing

there? I was just giving the nephew a ring—giving him a ring, you know, to see did he sell the old hotel we've had on our books for . . . What the hell are you looking at me like that for? For Christ's sake, a man's entitled to look after his business, isn't he? You've a rotten, suspicious mind, Moloney, that's what's wrong with you: you think everyone's as corrupt as you are—that's your trouble . . . And for a man in public life it's—it's—

MOLONEY

Is he reliable?

RYAN

I don't know what you're—

MOLONEY

Delia's brother—the teacher—Kieran—can you trust him?

RYAN

You're drunk.

MOLONEY

Because if he talks we're both in the soup.

RYAN

Both?

MOLONEY

You and I.

RYAN

Jaysus, you're a right rat!

MOLONEY
Because we're in partnership as from now.

RYAN
You were always a bloody gangster, Moloney.

MOLONEY
And if one blows the gaff we're all . . . embarrassed.
So let's be meticulous. I take it Declan's reliable? (*Pause.*)
Well, *is* he?

RYAN
He's my nephew, isn't he?

MOLONEY
That's the point.

RYAN
Watch it, Moloney: I'm not—

MOLONEY
And his wife, Delia.

RYAN
She's a good girl.

MOLONEY
And Kieran, the straw man?

RYAN
He'll be paid. He won't talk. He's honest.

MOLONEY

Good. But don't use him again. Too easily traced. And it's madness to buy up whole stretches in one area. What we do is pick our places carefully and far apart. And if any questions are asked . . .

He gets a signal from RYAN *to stop.* NASH *has entered.*

NASH

Excuse me, sir . . .

RYAN

Quite all right, Roger. We're just—just finishing up here. Did you forget something?

NASH

No, sir. I've been inside all the time.

He goes straight to the desk and ostentatiously switches off the intercom.

NASH

You left the intercom switched on.

RYAN

Did I?

NASH *relaxes in a seat.*

NASH

And if I may make a suggestion, gentlemen—

MOLONEY

I'm off, F.X. See you in the—

RYAN

Just a second, Mick. Yes, Roger—your suggestion? (*He has poured himself a drink.*)

NASH

May I? Thank you. You're really much more expert in these things than I, sir, but couldn't we do something like this? When the government comes to vest this land, the price per acre will be determined by the current market value of that land or of similar land in a similar locality. Isn't this the standard of assessment?

MOLONEY

I really must be off.

NASH

So if we were to form—

RYAN

We?

NASH

—were to form two companies. Not ourselves personally, of course, F.X. The first company, Company A, could acquire the land cheaply, sell it at a substantial profit to Company B, who would sell it back at a profit to Company A, who would sell it back at a profit to Company B. (*To* MOLONEY) Francis Ferdinand had excellent taste.

MOLONEY

What land? What are you talking about?

NASH

Please, Mick. And in that way, when the government comes to vesting and payment, the current market value of the lands they would wish to acquire would be very enhanced indeed. And honor would demand that you pay yourselves a fair price, wouldn't it?

RYAN

You're clever, Nash.

NASH

Not really, F.X. This sort of thing's done all the time, as you know well. But this method does augment our profit margin. And since there's now a three-way split, I do urge you to consider my proposal seriously. (*Smelling his drink.*) Very smooth on the tongue.

Pause.

RYAN

Sit down, Mick.

MOLONEY *sits.*

CURTAIN

ACT THREE

Three weeks later. Morning. The eve of the inauguration of the Mundy Scheme. The old map has been replaced by a new one: and the area blacked in by MOLONEY *is now covered in decorative miniature flags.*

  RYAN *is on the phone. He is fully recovered, well dressed, **and** obviously on top of things.*

  NASH *is sharpening a pencil at his own desk.*

RYAN

Yes, Captain—that's very interesting, yes, the music . . . But tell me, Captain, er—er . . . I'm sorry—you'll have to speak up; this line's bad. (*Covers phone. To* NASH) Captain What-what-what?

NASH

Sweeney.

RYAN

That's much better, Captain Sweeney—loud and clear now. Could I have those names again? (*To* NASH) When are the TV people due?

NASH

Any minute.

RYAN

I'd be very happy to leave the choice of music in your competent hands, Captain; as long as it's suitably funereal without making it positively morose. We don't want to become a nation of necrophiliacs, do we, ha-ha-ha . . . Fine, fine . . . The National Anthem, yes, the Dead March, yes. Both short and sweet, Captain . . . "Nearer My God to Thee"—why not?

NASH

What if your first consignment's all Jews from the Bronx?

RYAN

(*Quickly*) And why not just limit it to the Dead March and the Anthem? Keep it brief. It's funereal, after all, not a fleadh . . . Thank you, Captain Sweeney . . . Goodbye. (*Hangs up.*) They'll want me to polish their bloody instruments for them next. Any news from the House?

NASH

Mahon's still on his feet defending the Scheme.

RYAN

Good God. (*On intercom*) Sally, get through to the House—Moloney, Hogan, anybody—and tell them for God's sake flag Mahon down. And, Sally, if Boyle's there, I want to see him.

NASH

(*Presenting papers*) Your TV speech broken into paragraphs.

RYAN

Thanks.

NASH

A German reporter called: wanted your views on the past crisis and the prospects for the future.

RYAN

I can't see anybody until late after—

NASH

I spoke to him. Said it gave you great personal satisfaction to hear the wheels of industry rolling again; and now all hands must turn with fresh zeal, vigor, and dedication to the national plow; and that with tomorrow's ceremony vast new horizons of opportunity and prosperity were opening up.

RYAN

Roger, when my views are sought on the state of the nation—

NASH

Would you have said something different, F.X.? That you were sorry to see the strike over? That it was naughty of you to silence the mighty strike leader, Curley McMurray, by threatening to expose his affair with the Minister of Labor's daughter-in-law? All I did, F.X., was to talk the same crap as you.

RYAN

One of these days, Nash, you're going to hang yourself.

NASH

(*Answering house phone*) And if I do, Prime Minister, we'll swing together. Yes? . . . Sorry. He's not available at the moment, Sally. (*Hangs up.*) The Gaelic League again. Fourth time this morning. They want at least 75 percent of the burial services conducted in Irish. (*Passing across a paper*) And this is a "passionate protest" from David MacAteer.

RYAN

Who's he?

NASH

Tch-tch-tch. You really are a Philistine, F.X. Ireland's leading poet. Describes you rather wittily as a "black, obscene Dracula."

RYAN

Very witty indeed. That's all those gets can do—mock and sneer and knock down! How are the papers?

NASH

Ours says we're on the threshold of a great new era; theirs says we're now legally dead; and *The Times* pleads for—

RYAN

A period of calm and reflection.

NASH

—for the protection of the black-tailed godwit.

RYAN

The Archbishop?

NASH

A bird. (*Answering phone*) Yes? . . . (*To* RYAN) The TV people are here.

RYAN

Hold them for a second.

NASH

(*Into phone*) In a minute.

RYAN

Would you close the door, Roger . . . please . . .

NASH *does this.* RYAN *takes an envelope from his wall safe.*

I want you to do something for me. I was to have given these papers to Declan this morning, but I can't get away now, and I don't want him to come here. It's the deeds for 200 acres northwest of Ballina.

NASH

Our empire has grown in the last three weeks, F.X.

RYAN

He'll be in the downstairs bar of the Imperial Hotel.

NASH

Where?

RYAN

The Imperial. It's in Dock Lane.

NASH

Sounds lovely.

RYAN

If he's not there, wait till he comes. Tell him everything's in hand—

NASH

I'm taking your word for that.

RYAN

—and that he'll get his money before the end of the week. And for heaven's sake impress on him again on no account pay for anything by check.

NASH

No-risk Ryan, the Honest Auctioneer.

RYAN

Put it in your inside pocket. It's your future you're carrying with you.

NASH

I'll be careful. Don't worry. Incidentally—no, I haven't forgotten anything—I need some more petty cash.

RYAN

Again?

NASH

I'm acquiring expensive tastes.

RYAN

Three days ago I gave—

NASH

Twenty pounds will do. A drop in the ocean to you, Mr. Ryan.

RYAN *stares at him momentarily, then opens his wallet.*

RYAN

You've become a real jolly Roger.

NASH

That's cruel.

RYAN

And this can't go on—you know that.

NASH

(*Taking money*) Thank you. It'll stop when our investments start paying dividends . . . cross my bones. (*Leaving*) I probably won't get back until after lunch.

RYAN

Why not?

NASH

As we used to say in school: "because; that's the why."
You'll manage?

RYAN

Pull the door after you, Roger.

NASH *leaves.* RYAN *pauses for a second, then checks whether the intercom is switched off, then lifts phone and dials.*

Commissioner McLaughlin, please . . . Vincent? F.X.
here. How's the big heart? . . . Good, good . . . Fine
again, Vince, thanks: making my first public appearance
at tomorrow's big do. And I want to congratulate you on
a magnificent job of work over the past few months;
really first-rate; a very difficult job beautifully handled.
In fact, I'm going to thank you publicly . . . Not at all,
I mean every word of it . . . Look, Vince, I'm in a spot
of bother; can you help me? . . . That's very kind of
you; I appreciate that very much, Vince. I'll tell you
what it is. My private secretary, young chap, Roger Nash
. . . Of course you know him. Well, not to put a tooth in
it, Vince, he's got himself into some sort of a mess . . .
I'm damned if I know, Vince, and all I do know is that
he's spending a lot more than he's earning . . . No, he's
not a gambler; but there was some whisper—I'm sure it's
only gossip—but someone did hint at drug-pushing. That
may or may not be true; but this morning, Vince, an

envelope containing £150 disappeared from my safe . . . About the drugs? No evidence whatever, except that for the past four or five weeks every Wednesday at about this time he invents some excuse to go downtown and some-one said he's been seen in that sleazy downstairs bar of the Imperial Hotel . . . Would you, Vince? God, that's decent of you . . . Look, Vince, when you lift him, if he has the money on him—well, with the Mundy Scheme opening tomorrow, it could be embarrassing if any publicity were to . . . Exactly, Vince, exactly; as discreetly as you can . . . Terribly distressing; and God alone knows what dirt he'll fling at me . . . Great, great . . . Mary and the kids all well? Oh, by the way, Vince, don't be too . . . stern with Nash. Poor chap never had much of a chance: father was a drunk and the mother was found dead in her bath . . . Oh, I thought you knew the family . . . Thanks again, Vince. God bless. God bless. (*Hangs up. Pours himself a short drink.*)

(*Into intercom*) I'll see the TV people now, Sally.

While he is waiting for them to come in, he combs his hair, adjusts his tie, and assumes his hearty public manner. SALLY *opens the door and introduces the TV crew.*

SALLY

The television people, Mr. Ryan.

RYAN

I'm sorry to have kept you waiting.

SALLY

Miss Toye, the producer; Mr. Sean O'Grady; and Mr. Tony Hanlan, Mr. Ryan.

RYAN

(*Shakes hands.*) How are you? How are you? Sally, see that we are not disturbed.

SALLY *exits.*

Very kind of you to come on such short notice. O'Grady —you're not one of the O'Gradys of Rathmore, are you?

O'GRADY

I'm the son of Tony O'Grady.

RYAN

For God's sake. Big Tony! Many's the dance Tony and I cycled to together in the old days. And every girl I ever took out he wiped my eye—and you can tell him I still hold it against him! How is he? Is he well?

OWEN, *the sound man, enters.*

How are you, son?

OWEN

Fine, thanks, Mr. Ryan.

RYAN

(*To* O'GRADY, *cameraman*) Would you ever do me a favor,

son? Keep the camera directly on my face, because if you move the least bit to the side, all the viewers'll see is the big nose. (*To* MISS TOYE) D'you want to put powder and stuff on me, love?

MISS TOYE

You're lovely as you are.

RYAN

There's a girl will go far—knows how to make an ugly old bachelor happy. You should be in politics, child. (*Sharply*) This goes out tonight?

MISS TOYE

Immediately before the news.

RYAN

(*Innocently*) And tell me—is that a good time?

MISS TOYE

It's the time you asked for, Mr. Ryan—peak viewing.

RYAN

Oh well, sure that's fine. Now we're all happy. (*Sits behind desk and glances over notes.*) As soon as you boys are ready, we'll start rolling.

O'GRADY

Mr. Ryan, would you mind very much moving a little to the left: and, Pat, if you could rearrange some of that stuff.

RYAN

Sean, me aul son, if you start fussing—I know it's your job and I know nothing about it—but you'll get me all floostered, and d'you know what'll happen to me then? I'll start stammering; and she'll bust her sides giggling at me; and we'll ruin the whole thing.

MISS TOYE

(*Moving phone*) That's better now.

RYAN

All set?

O'GRADY

I still haven't a straight—

RYAN

How long have I got? Five minutes?

MISS TOYE

That's what's scheduled. All right, Tony?

HANLAN

Okay.

O'GRADY

Lights, please, Tony. I'm afraid, Mr. Ryan, I must ask you to move a little to the left so that we don't catch—

RYAN

I may overrun by a few seconds. But if I do, Jack Hartigan won't mind. (*To* o'GRADY) He's your immediate boss, isn't he?

O'GRADY

He is.

RYAN

Thought so. Right. Let's go.

OWEN

Pat, can I have a voice level.

MISS TOYE

Could we have a few words for voice level, Mr. Ryan?

RYAN

Aon, do, tri, ceathair, cuig, se, seacht . . .

MISS TOYE

How's that, Owen?

OWEN

Fine, thanks.

MISS TOYE

Right, Sean.

O'GRADY

Camera.

OWEN

Speed.

MISS TOYE

In your own time, Mr. Ryan.

RYAN

I want to talk to you tonight because I feel that this is a momentous occasion in the history of our country. As you are all painfully aware, we have just emerged from a dark night of turmoil and distress. We have seen our nation rent by strife and dissention, as a result of which our economy was hurled into disarray and our personal lives disrupted and disorganized.

Indeed, for a time it looked as if the process of democratic government was going to be routed by the elements of anarchy and destruction. But when the decent people of Ireland finally realized that everything they loved and cherished was about to be wrenched from them, they said, "No! Let's stand up against this insanity, this evil. Let's show the world that an ancient and cultured nation will never ever espouse Godlessness." And, thank God, the decent people of Ireland prevailed. And before I turn my back on this unhappy past, I would like to pay generous tribute to you for your courage, to my colleagues for their unswerving loyalty, and to the police force under Commissioner McLaughlin for their firmness and impartiality in very difficult circumstances.

But now we look to tomorrow and to the future. And it is a future—and I don't say this casually or without due deliberation—it is a future of immeasurable potential. As you already know, the realization of that potential begins at noon tomorrow when Church and state dignitaries from all over the free world will congregate at Dublin Airport to bless and welcome the first installment, as it were, of our new inheritance. We shall then proceed west, to Achill, and there it will be my privilege to turn the first sod that will herald the first day of our economic spring. But tomorrow's ceremonies are merely a beginning. Next week and the week after and the week after that, more and more planes will fill the Irish skies, bringing greater prosperity and peace and fulfillment, not only to Achill, but to Clare and Connemara and Sligo and Leitrin and Roscommon and ultimately to all these western areas that have suffered too long from neglect.

I would be doing less than my honest duty tonight if I were to avoid using the words "cemetery" and "grave" and "death"—words that our opponents keep chanting. Ireland, they say, is to be an international graveyard, a burial ground, a place of death. And quite frankly I find this puzzling. Is the honorable interment of God's deceased in some way shameful just because they are not our own deceased? Is it despicable to provide the last facilities for these who have gone to their eternal reward? Is it unbecoming for the Church Militant to practice one of the charitable works of mercy for the Church Triumphant? Or has your government embarked on some scandalous and infamous path? May I answer these questions in this way—and in a way I know would have been endorsed by John F. Kennedy and good Pope John himself. The days of parochial, provincial parish-pump thinking are over. Either you proudly proclaim your membership of the global village—or you die. No country can live in isolation. We are all dependent and interdependent. Commerce, trade, and business have made us all brothers. Let me put it to you this way: we do not refuse industrial machinery because it is made in Germany; nor do we turn away tourists from England and France and America just because they are English and French and American. Or are we now suddenly to abandon this basic principle? Do the obscurantists want us to stop driving cars that haven't been assembled in Ireland? And is tomorrow's ceremony in some way alien to the plans and policies that this government has devised and pursued against all opposition? If I thought for one second that the answers to these questions was yes, I would not be talking to you in your good homes tonight.

When I want to know what Ireland is thinking, I go to a secluded spot and look into my heart. And my heart tells me that we have finally come into our patrimony. The west's awake. Ireland's awake. Opportunity abounds.

Opportunity for the worker to earn a decent wage that is realistically related to current prices. Opportunity for the

Church to show that Irish Christianity once more leads the world in ecumenism and charity. Opportunity for our renowned artists and writers and poets to forget the gray past and celebrate the new dawn with happy panegyric and joyful dirge and wholesome, hearty plays. Opportunity for all of us to create the Ireland the idealists of 1916 gave their lives for. As Padraic Henry Pearce wrote: "We are young. And God has given us strength and courage, and counsel. May he give us victory." Good night and God's blessing on all of you.

MISS TOYE

Cut, Sean? . . . Sound?

O'GRADY *and* OWEN *signify all is okay technically.*

RYAN

Well. There we are. How did we do for time?

MISS TOYE

Six and a half minutes.

RYAN

Was it, really? And I was only warming up at the very end. How did it sound, son?

HANLAN

Very impressive, Mr. Ryan.

RYAN

D'you hear him—"very impressive"! Nothing impresses

you cynics. Can I get you anything—a drink? tea? coffee? (*Rapidly*) No, I suppose you're dashing off to grill some other poor innocent. (*Dismissing with handshakes*) Thank you very much for coming here and for being so patient with me. Give my best wishes to your father, Sean—and to Jack Hartigan.

o'grady

I will, sir.

ryan

Thank you, Tony.

hanlan

Pleasure.

o'grady, hanlan, *and* owen *exit.*

ryan

I didn't catch your Christian name, Miss Toye.

miss toye

Pat.

ryan

Pat? Now isn't that a pretty name for a pretty girl, eh? And what age are you, Pat?

miss toye

Twenty-two, Mr. Ryan.

RYAN

My God—only twenty-two.

MOLONEY *dashes into the room. He is very agitated.*

Michael, I'd like you to meet Miss Toye. Miss Toye, Michael Moloney.

MISS TOYE

How do you do.

RYAN

Miss Toye tells me she's only twenty-two. And holding down an important job. And I see you're engaged too— lucky man.

MOLONEY

F.X., I've got to speak to you immediately.

RYAN

Oh! Will you excuse us, Miss Toye?

MISS TOYE

Certainly. (*As she exits*) Goodbye, Mr. Ryan.

RYAN

Goodbye, Pat. (*He closes the door behind her and turns to face* MOLONEY.)

MOLONEY

Nash has been lifted.

RYAN

What?

MOLONEY

By the Special Branch.

RYAN

You're joking. He's here—in the office.

MOLONEY

I'm telling you, man. The House is agog with the news.

RYAN

(*On house phone*) Send Roger in, please. (*Pause.*) How long ago?

MOLONEY

What in the name of God has the bloody fool done?

RYAN

(*Into phone*) It doesn't matter, Sally. Thank you. (*Hangs up.*)

MOLONEY

And if he talks, F.X., if the bastard spills the beans, we're both ruined! And why the Special Branch—why not the ordinary guards?

RYAN

Calm down, Mick, will you?

MOLONEY

And why haven't they notified you? They wouldn't dare arrest your private secretary without at least telling you first—unless they knew about—

RYAN

Will you shut up! (*Passes bottle.*) Pour yourself a drink and get a grip on yourself.

MOLONEY

We're up to the neck, F.X. I'm telling you. I know it.

RYAN

(*On phone*) Get me the Commissioner.

MOLONEY

For Christ's sake, man, are you out of your—!

RYAN

Just shut up, will you, and let me handle this. Pour yourself a drink and get a grip on yourself.

MOLONEY

Did he ever have anything in writing, any papers, deeds?

RYAN

None.

MOLONEY

Checks—copies of transfers?

RYAN

D'you think I'm a fool?

MOLONEY

But he'll talk—he'll blurt it all—

RYAN

(*On phone*) Vincent? Vince, Mick Moloney has just come in to me . . . He's fine, Vince, fine . . . I'll tell him, surely . . . Look, Vince, he tells me that Roger Nash . . .

MOLONEY

You see!

RYAN

Arrested? Good God!

MOLONEY

I told you!

RYAN

Yes . . . I see . . . Yes . . . Did he make a statement?

MOLONEY

Did he? Did he? What did he say?

RYAN

How much? . . . In notes?

MOLONEY

Was it checks?

RYAN

My God, that's awful, Vince, awful. Look, Vince, with the ceremony tomorrow and everything, could you hold your hand for, say, forty-eight hours? Or, better still, could you come and see me some time this afternoon?

MOLONEY

You're mad, F.X.!

RYAN

No, no, I had no idea at all: just devastating, absolutely incredible . . . Good man, Vince; I'm very grateful to you . . . See you after lunch. (*Hangs up.*) God!

MOLONEY

What did he say?

Phone rings. RYAN *lifts receiver.*

RYAN

Yes? (*Pause.*) Give me a minute.

MOLONEY

F.X., for Christ's sake—!

RYAN

Keep your voice down. Boyle's outside. (*He goes to the safe and glances in.*)

MOLONEY

What's happening? Has he talked?

RYAN

He was arrested in the bar of the Imperial and taken straight to the Castle. When they searched him, they found £150 in an envelope, as well as a list of names and addresses.

MOLONEY

A hundred and fifty pounds. Nash?

RYAN

Lifted from here, obviously.

MOLONEY

But how did they know? You didn't—?

RYAN

So far, they haven't got a word out of him.

MOLONEY

Names and addresses of what?

RYAN

Drug addicts. Looks as if Nash was a pusher.

MOLONEY

Nash? You're not serious!

RYAN

Vince thinks he may well be a key figure.

MOLONEY

(*Dumfounded*) For God's sake! Polite Roger! (*Anxious again*) But when they start squeezing him, he's bound to talk then and—

RYAN

He'll try to incriminate us all, won't he? He'll do anything to save himself, won't he?

MOLONEY

And he'll tell that we've bought 5,000 acres right along—

RYAN

Of course he will. And God knows what other lies he'll invent. But Vince knows the type. Vince understands. Probably won't even charge him.

MOLONEY

He has to charge him! He can't hold him if he doesn't charge him!

RYAN

Must he? I never understood the workings of the law. I suppose you're right.

MOLONEY

In fact, you'll have to bring the case! It's your money, isn't it?

RYAN

Charge my own private secretary? Oh, I could never do that.

MOLONEY

The police will insist, F.X.!

RYAN *moves beside* MOLONEY *and talks to him as if he were a child.*

RYAN

Wouldn't it be so much more simple, Mick, if the police were to . . . chastise him for being a bold boy and then let him take himself away to Tasmania or somewhere— so much better for Nash himself and for you and for me and for the country. Wouldn't that be the simplest solution?

MOLONEY *suddenly knows.*

RYAN

(*Moving away*) At least, that's what I'll suggest to Vincent this afternoon. Nobody wants to harass a poor unfortunate clerk that hasn't a friend or relative in the world —isn't that true?

MOLONEY

You are a goddamn crafty bastard, F. X. Ryan.

RYAN

Crafty?

MOLONEY

And by God I admire you.

RYAN

Let's say we admire one another, Mick. (*Intercom*) Ask
Mr. Boyle to come in. (*To* MOLONEY) So now we're back
where we started.

MOLONEY

A two-way split again.

RYAN

And we can trust one another.

MOLONEY

We can. Can't we?

RYAN

Of course we can.

MOLONEY

Of course.

BOYLE *enters.*

BOYLE

Morning, F.X. Morning, Michael.

RYAN

How are you, Neil?

MOLONEY

I must run. Cocktails at the Albanian Embassy at 11:30. 'Bye, Neil.

BOYLE

Goodbye.

MOLONEY

I'll phone you later, F.X.

RYAN

Do that, Mick.

MOLONEY *goes.*

BOYLE

What's this rumor about Roger Nash?

RYAN

What did you hear?

BOYLE

That he's been arrested.

RYAN

It's true.

BOYLE

Why? What for?

RYAN

Peddling drugs. Isn't it wonderful?

BOYLE

Drugs? Go on!

RYAN

And he has broken down and confessed all—and that's it, Neil.

BOYLE

Between ourselves, F.X., I'm not surprised. Never liked the fellow.

RYAN

That's interesting. Why not?

BOYLE

Not so much that I didn't like him; I just didn't trust him.

RYAN

Wasn't that shrewd of you, Neil.

BOYLE

Just—just an intuition. I'm seldom wrong.

RYAN

He fooled me up to here, I must admit. So there you are . . . (*Briskly*) You've just come from the House. How's the debate going?

BOYLE

Mahon spoke for eighty-five minutes.

RYAN

Was it terrible?

BOYLE

Most of it. He said, "Even if we did sell half the country to America, we got top prices for it."

RYAN

He really will have to be muzzled.

BOYLE

And he ended up almost in tears: "If only my mother had lived to see this day."

RYAN

What's done is done. Neil, something I want you to do for me.

BOYLE

If I can.

RYAN

The bloody hierarchy is having second thoughts about communal services and about blessing the crematorium.

BOYLE

I thought that was all arranged.

RYAN

They now say they consented only to "joint services with fellow Christians." They draw the line at Jews, Mohammedans, and whatnot.

BOYLE

But the Cardinal *will* be there tomorrow, won't he?

RYAN

Catch him missing it. But what I want you to convey to him through his secretary—what's his name?

BOYLE

Father Coughlin.

RYAN

That's him. Let him know that Mundy Incorporated are working out a scale of professional fees for clergymen of all denominations. You'll be handling it. And you can let Coughlin know that he'll get the lion's share—or put it whatever polite way you like.

BOYLE

I'll call him immediately.

RYAN

That'll take care of their scruples.

BOYLE

Decent chap, Coughlin. Same class right through Clongowes. Anything else I can do?

RYAN

(*Abstracted*) Mmm?

BOYLE

Something worrying you, F.X.?

RYAN

Mick Moloney . . . Thinking about Mick.

BOYLE

Anything the matter?

RYAN

Why should a man tell me a deliberate and pointless lie?
Why say he's going to a reception in the Albanian Embassy
when that reception was yesterday morning?

BOYLE

Maybe he's getting absent-minded like me.

RYAN

Tell me, Neil, have you ever met the Ambassador's wife?

BOYLE

Madame Legouis? Once or twice.

RYAN

Is it true that she's . . . (*Laughs disarmingly*) . . . as
our old P.P. down at home used to say, "lascivious?"

BOYLE

I really wouldn't know, F.X. . . . I've heard stories, of
course. But you know the way that Embassy crowd gos-
sips. Why do you ask?

RYAN

(*After a second of pretended consideration*) Well, I'll take you into my confidence. May I?

BOYLE

Please . . . please.

RYAN

Mick is being . . . to put it at its best . . . indiscreet.

BOYLE

Drinking?

RYAN *shakes his head.*

Women?

RYAN

(*Rapidly*) Who told you?

BOYLE

No one; I'm only guess—

RYAN

You know about him and this Albanian woman?

BOYLE

I really never heard a word—

RYAN

You've seen them together, have you?

BOYLE

I *promise* you, F.X., this is all news to—

RYAN

Naturally, I'd be the last to hear. But it must stop—it must stop! A scandal in the Cabinet at this critical juncture and we're all washed up.

BOYLE

I'm sure you're exaggerating, F.X. Moloney's no fool. What evidence have you got?

RYAN

Evidence?

BOYLE

Of indiscretion.

RYAN *gives him his patient, weary smile and puts his arm around* BOYLE'*s shoulder. Ushers him to the door.*

RYAN

None. Not a scrap. But in our profession, Neil, if you wait until conclusive evidence is presented to you, you're a dead man. So what the provident politician does is . . . he goes looking for it, and it's always there, Neil, it's always there. God bless, Neil, God bless.

BOYLE *exits, and as* RYAN *turns,*

THE CURTAIN FALLS

Scene 2

The following night. BOYLE, MAHON, HOGAN, *and* MOLONEY *have returned from the west. They are dressed in morning suits; top hats and coats are lying across the couch.*

They have been drinking sporadically all evening since the Achill ceremony, but only BOYLE *is really drunk. He sits down front by himself in a private reverie and now and then raises his glass to an imaginary colleague beside him.*

RYAN *is opening a bottle of champagne and insists they all have some, even though they already have glasses in their hands. There is a big cheer and pop of a champagne cork.*

RYAN

They don't make this stuff in your constituency, Charlie.

HOGAN

Is it champagne?

RYAN

Well, it was a big day, wasn't it? And we deserve it, don't we?

MAHON

Will you all keep quitet! I want to say something.

MOLONEY

Speech from Deputy Mahon. Silence, please!

RYAN

That's better. That's more like it.

MAHON

Will you listen to what I have to say?

RYAN

Try that, Charlie.

HOGAN

I'm as full as a pig, God spare you.

RYAN

What have you got to say, Dan?

HOGAN

My Auntie Nellie'll be very vexed with me.

BOYLE

(*Softly, in private toast*) To my Auntie Nellie.

MAHON

When the Archbishop stood up there before all them foreigners—

RYAN

(*Giving* MAHON *a glass*) There you are.

MAHON

—and spoke in four different languages, he was as good as any Pope: and by Jaysus I was proud of him!

HOGAN

Lovely, F.X. Very nice.

RYAN

Some more?

MAHON

So I went straight up to him.

MOLONEY

Then every TV camera was on you.

MAHON

—and I said—

MOLONEY

Good for a thousand votes.

MAHON

(*To* MOLONEY) Will you shut up!

HOGAN

(*Drinking*) Lovely.

MOLONEY

And you said . . . ?

MAHON

"Your Grace," I said, "the electorate of Upper Sloblands is behind you to a man." And he said to me, "Daniel," he said, "the Church depends on good men like you." **And he's right. Isn't he right, F.X.?**

RYAN

Right on the nail.

MAHON

The biggest day in my life— (*Discovering glass in his hand*) What in the name of God is this?

HOGAN

What about Neil? Have you none for Neil?

RYAN

Coming, coming.

MOLONEY

Some bugger in Castlebar has renamed his pub the Post Mortem.

HOGAN

I heard two Achill men talking—

MAHON

I want to say something more.

BOYLE

To Achill.

RYAN

Have a go at that, Neil.

BOYLE

Merci beaucoup.

MAHON

Listen to me—

HOGAN

And one fellow says to the other—pointing out with a stick—"My meadow there's London and the upper field's Brooklyn."

MOLONEY

(*Quietly, as* RYAN *hands him a glass*) It went well, didn't it?

RYAN

Very well.

MAHON

It was when they were saying the prayers—I thought, by Jaysus, I was going to cry.

RYAN

(*To* MAHON) The music does that to you, Dan.

HOGAN

God Almighty, wasn't it sweet, eh?

RYAN

That band's being reserved for the Mundy Scheme. They'll be stationed in Galway and that's all they'll do.

HOGAN

And did you see all those fine young Mayo lads standing to attention with their shovels, waiting to fill in the graves?

RYAN

Returned emigrants, most of them; did you know that?

MAHON

Bloody marvelous.

HOGAN

"The upper field's Brooklyn."

BOYLE

To Brooklyn.

RYAN

Did you ever in your lives see as many TV and newspaper men?

MOLONEY

I saw a reporter from Ceylon.

MAHON

And I'll bet my shirt that when the *Western Gazette* comes out next Friday it won't even mention my name!

HOGAN

What's he talking about?

RYAN

They'll have you on the front page, Dan!

MAHON

Like bloody hell! D'you know that when my mother died —may God be good to her—they put me in with the *also present or represented!*

HOGAN

Who did?

MAHON

And me her only gosling!

HOGAN

Where's Mick? Where's the Minister for External Affairs?

MOLONEY

Here, Charlie.

HOGAN

(*Holding up glass*) God Almighty, Mick— (*To others*) Only for Mick Moloney, lads, this day might never have been. Eh?

MAHON

Now you're talking.

HOGAN

Only for Mick, we might all be out footing turf at this minute.

MOLONEY

    We pulled it off, Charlie, didn't we?

HOGAN

    Pulled it off? God Almighty, man, you've made Ireland into a world power. And Ireland will remember that.

MAHON

    A born leader, Mick.

HOGAN

    The best brain in the party.

Momentary silence as MOLONEY *and* RYAN *stare at one another.* RYAN *breaks the moment with a hearty:*

RYAN

    A toast to Mick Moloney, boys. The Minister for External Affairs.

MAHON

    And to all of us—for we're a bloody great team.

They drink to this. RYAN *suddenly breaks in.*

RYAN

    It'll soon be time for the news. You want to see yourselves on the TV, don't you?

BOYLE *jumps to his feet and looks about desperately for an exit.*

HOGAN

Are you all right, Neillie boy?

BOYLE

Where? Where—

HOGAN

F.X.!

RYAN

Up the stairs, first on the right.

BOYLE *dashes off.*

HOGAN

Will you make it, Neillie? D'you want a hand?

MAHON

Everything went like a dream—except for one thing.

RYAN

What was that?

MAHON

The students with their bloody placards and banners—
they let the side down.

MOLONEY

They did no harm. The guards had their measure.

MAHON

I'll tell you now—I was affronted.

RYAN

Democracy, Daniel. Freedom of speech and all that.

MAHON

If that's what an education does to you, here's to ignorance.

HOGAN

What's he talking about?

RYAN

The news will be on in a minute.

As they gather around the set:

MOLONEY

The tourist boys were telling me they've got two big conventions lined up for the autumn.

MAHON

They've got three.

MOLONEY

I heard about two.

MAHON

The World Alliance of Morticians . . .

RYAN

(*To* HOGAN) Another drop?

HOGAN

A taste.

MAHON

The European Florists Association . . .

HOGAN

(*To* F.X. *as he pours*) Steady—steady—

MAHON

And the International Conference of E.S.P.

HOGAN

Of what?

MAHON

Extra-Sensory Perception.

HOGAN

Are they colored people?

MAHON

Colored! Jaysus, I'm working with thicks!

MOLONEY

(*At door*) Come on down and see the news, Neil.

RYAN

(*To* MAHON) Come over, Dan. You'll see nothing from there.

MAHON

"Are they colored people?"

HOGAN

I don't know what he's (MAHON) talking about.

MAHON

JAYSUS!

MOLONEY

(*To* BOYLE, *as he enters*) How are you feeling, Neil?

RYAN

He's looking fine.

BOYLE

(*Teeth chattering*) Splendid . . . really splendid . . .

HOGAN

Sit down, Neil.

MAHON

Colored!

RYAN

Shhh. Quiet, boys, quiet. Here we are.

MOLONEY

Turn up the sound a bit.

ANNOUNCER

. . . at the inauguration of the Mundy Scheme.

MAHON

Thicks!

ANNOUNCER

Dignitaries of Church and state and a crowd estimated at
seven thousand were at Dublin Airport today to meet two
planes chartered by Mundy Incorporated which arrived
within minutes of one another from New York and Paris.

MAHON

(*Shouts*) There's the bastard students.

ANNOUNCER

The freight was unloaded onto a fleet of waiting funeral
cars which were decked with flowers and flags of the par-
ticipating nations.

MAHON

God, Charlie, the coffins are a credit to you.

HOGAN

Thank you, Daniel.

MOLONEY

Shhh.

HOGAN

Burmese oak—

ANNOUNCER

The procession, headed by a cavalcade of gardai and cavalry, then drove slowly through the city, where the streets were lined with sightseers, many of whom cried as the three-mile-long column passed by.

MAHON

There's you, Neil.

BOYLE

And F.X.

HOGAN

And me! God Almighty, with my mouth hanging open!

ANNOUNCER

When they reached the general post office in O'Connell Street, the procession halted and a minute's silence was observed.

RYAN

There you are, Dan.

MAHON

There—where—where—where am I?

RYAN

Too late.

MAHON

The hoors!

ANNOUNCER

When the entourage arrived at the international cemetery in Achill Island, the burials were conducted in batches of twenty, while clergymen of different denominations recited prayers in Irish, English, French, and German.

The phone rings. RYAN *answers it.* MOLONEY *watches him.*

HOGAN

Christ, isn't that a spectacle, eh?

RYAN

Just a moment.

ANNOUNCER

At the conclusion of the ceremony Mr. Mundy said that it was unfair to suggest, as some people had suggested, that wherever she stretched her tentacles, America spread decadence and death and decay. All Americans loved Ireland dearly and he was confident that more and more of them would settle here permanently.

RYAN

(*To* MOLONEY) For you. A woman with a foreign accent.

MOLONEY—*with some embarrassment before* RYAN's *cold eye—goes to the phone.* RYAN *watches him as he answers it in mumbled tones.*

ANNOUNCER

The services were concluded with the sounding of the last post.

All three coincide: MOLONEY *on phone;* RYAN *watching him; the sounding of the last post.*

MAHON

Bloody beautiful.

ANNOUNCER

Later tonight we will bring you a filmed account of to-day's complete ceremonies.

MAHON *is crying.*

RYAN

(*Switching off*) And that's it. An historic event. And we created it.

HOGAN

By God, it was impressive.

BOYLE

And chastening . . . Very emotive.

They move away from the set—except MAHON, *who is weeping helplessly.*

MOLONEY *goes to* RYAN.

MOLONEY

D'you mind if I slip away, F.X.?

RYAN

Anything wrong?

MOLONEY

That was our little *au pair* maid. One of the kids fell in the yard and the wife's afraid he's broken his arm.

RYAN

Let me call a doctor for you.

MOLONEY

No—no—no—no; she's probably panicked. Okay?

RYAN

Of course . . . of course.

MOLONEY

I'll not break up the party. See you tomorrow.

RYAN

God bless, Mick. Thanks for everything.

MOLONEY *picks up his hat and coat and leaves.*

HOGAN

Couldn't have been more tastefully done. I'll tell you boys: there's a proud group of 1916 fellows sitting up in heaven this night. God Almighty, they'll turn the place into

Croke Park. And the aul sticks'll be flashing and— (*He sees* MAHON *limp with grief.*) What's wrong, Dan?

MAHON

Leave me.

HOGAN

Danny boy, what's the matter with you?

MAHON

Leave me be.

BOYLE

I know exactly how he feels . . . exactly.

HOGAN

(*To* RYAN) What the hell's wrong with them?

RYAN

It's all right, Charlie.

HOGAN

(*Into* RYAN'*s ear*) What is it, F.X.?

RYAN

(*Sententiously*) There are times, Charles, when tears are no dishonor to a man. There are occasions when tears are right and fitting. (*He blows his nose and grips* MAHON'*s shuddering shoulder.*) God bless you, Dan. (*Now very briskly*) And now what about a wee drop before we break up?

MAHON *is already getting his coat.* BOYLE *copies him.*

HOGAN

Break up? Who's breaking up? It's early yet!

RYAN

Are you . . . Maybe you're right, too. We're all emotionally spent. (*He gets* HOGAN'*s coat and hands it to him.*)

MAHON

(*Almost inarticulate*) You know, F.X., don't you?

RYAN

Not a word, Dan.

MAHON

You understand, don't you?

RYAN

Not another word.

MAHON

The music and all those headstones and my poor mother
. . . (*He turns away.*)

RYAN

We're all . . . we're all too damned sentimental . . . Our
bloody ruination.

HOGAN

Be God and I was set for a long session!

RYAN

Charlie, you'll see Dan to his hotel?

HOGAN

My Auntie Nellie has a bed for him—if he can make it!

RYAN

Dan's a fighter. He can make it.

BOYLE

F.X., I'm sorry for . . . for making an exhibition of myself.

RYAN

You did nothing of the kind, Neil.

MAHON

God spare you, chief.

RYAN

And you, too, Dan Mahon.

MAHON

I want to . . . to . . . (*He can get no further. He dashes for the door. Exits.*)

RYAN

Safe home, Charles. See you in the morning.

HOGAN

I never saw a party end so quick in my life.

RYAN

There'll be another day.

HOGAN

I don't see what's wrong with tonight. (*He exits.*)

RYAN

And how are you feeling now, Neil?

BOYLE

I'm fine now, thank you.

RYAN

Neil, you're a man of considerable talent and perception. And now that your department is as good as out of the red, I've been turning over in my mind the possibility of employing your talents in some other sphere. You'd welcome a new challenge, wouldn't you?

BOYLE

As you know yourself, F.X., I took over Finance very reluctantly. It's not really my forte at all.

RYAN

And look at the job you make of it. Let's keep an open mind on this, shall we? . . . Just thinking aloud, random thoughts . . . Let me put it this way: supposing there was a vacancy in the Cabinet—let's say, for the sake of argument, let's say there was a vacancy in foreign affairs, where we could do with a bit of culture, a bit of class—would you be prepared to assume a new and challenging responsibility?

BOYLE

Michael Moloney's post? But—but—

RYAN

Just a thought—an idle speculation. We'll talk no more about it. Listen! D'you know I believe it's still raining. Have you an umbrella?

BOYLE

I—I—

RYAN

I'll call a taxi.

BOYLE

Please, F.X., please, I'd prefer to walk and clear my head and think about—

RYAN

(*Steering him out*) Fine, fine. Whatever you say. A breath of air'll do you good. Have a good long sleep, Neil. And thank you very sincerely for all your help. Invaluable.

BOYLE

I did my best, F.X.

RYAN

And your best is superb. God bless, Neil. See you in the morning. And if you don't feel like turning in, no harm done.

BOYLE

(*Great sincerity*) Thank you, F.X. Thank you very much.

RYAN *closes the door behind* BOYLE *and comes thoughtfully into the center of the room. He pours himself a drink, goes to the couch, sits down, and very slowly begins taking off his shoes.*

RYAN

(*To himself*) *Au pair* maid!

MRS. RYAN

(*Off*) Frankie!

RYAN

Yes, Mammy.

MRS. RYAN

Did you get rid of them?

RYAN

All gone, Mammy.

She enters. Dressed smartly for outside and carrying a shopping basket.

MRS. RYAN

Your breakfast's on the table. I'm going out for a few things.

RYAN

(*Dreamily*) It's nighttime.

MRS. RYAN

Hurry up. The toast's getting cold.

RYAN

They're taking all this stuff away tomorrow. We'll have the house to ourselves again.

MRS. RYAN

I was looking at you on TV. You were like . . . like a High King.

RYAN

Was I?

MRS. RYAN

And I was so proud of you. And the country's so proud of you.

RYAN

I'm naughty, Mammy.

MRS. RYAN

Indeed you're not.

RYAN

I am. Yes, I am.

MRS. RYAN

Well, if you do an odd bold thing, Frankie, it's for the sake of the country.

RYAN

Exactly.

MRS. RYAN

I'm going to pour your tea and then I'm just going to leave it to get cold. So come if you want or stay if you want. Because you'll only keep me late for the shops. (*She exits.*)

RYAN

I'll be straight up. (*He crosses to the phone, looks up a number, dials it.*) The Albanian Embassy? . . . Green Star Taxis here. Could you tell me, did a Mr. Moloney order a cab? . . . Mr. Moloney *is* there now, isn't he? . . . Oh, he's just *arrived* by taxi—that's probably the confusion. My mistake, thank you very much. Good night.

MRS. RYAN

Frankie.

RYAN

Coming, Mammy.

He lifts his shoes and goes slowly toward the door.

CURTAIN

The Mundy Scheme was first performed at the Olympia Theatre, Dublin, on June 10, 1969. It was directed by Donal Donnelly, with the following cast:

Roger Nash	PATRICK LAFFAN
Sally	OLIVIA SHANLEY
F. X. Ryan	GODFREY QUIGLEY
Neil Boyle	CECIL BARROR
Mrs. Ryan	MAY CLUSKEY
Michael Moloney	BARRY KEEGAN
Dan Mahon	MARTIN DEMPSEY
Charles Hogan	SEAMUS HEALY
Pat Toye	ITA D'ARCY
Sean O'Grady	CLIVE GERAGHTY
Tony Hanlan	JOHN AVER
Owen	MAURICE COONEY
The Singer	MARY COONEY
The Musician	SEAN POTTS
Prelude Announcer	SEAMUS FORDE